D0559826

All Things Considered

Books by Russell Baker

ALL THINGS CONSIDERED
NO CAUSE FOR PANIC
AN AMERICAN IN WASHINGTON

Russell Baker

all
things
considered

GREENWOOD PRESS, PUBLISHERS
WESTPORT, CONNECTICUT

973.92
B16a

Library of Congress Cataloging in Publication Data

Baker, Russell, 1925–
   All things considered.

      Reprint. Originally published: 1st ed. Philadelphia :
   Lippincott, 1965.
      A collection of articles from the author's New York
   times column.
      1. United States--Social life and customs--1945-1970
   --Anecdotes, facetiae, satire, etc. I. New York times.
   II. Title.
   [E169.02.B27 1981]   973.92   81-6883
   ISBN 0-313-22875-2 (lib. bdg.)   AACR2

Copyright © 1962, 1963, 1964, 1965 by The New York
Times Company.

This is a reprint of the 1965 J. B. Lippincott First Edition.

Reprinted with the permission of Harper & Row Publishers,
Inc.

Reprinted in 1981 by Greenwood Press
A division of Congressional Information Service, Inc.
88 Post Road West, Westport, Connecticut 06881

Printed in the United States of America

10 9 8 7 6 5 4 3 2 1

Contents

UNIVERSITY LIBRARIES
CARNEGIE-MELLON UNIVERSITY
PITTSBURGH, PENNSYLVANIA 15213

II

Life in the Great Society

Doomed, and what's new?

To think at a slow amble is hardly ever done these days. Most of us have lost the knack of it, if indeed we ever had it.

Right now, for example, there is really nothing around to get terribly excited about. Europe, which looked to be near the end of the road in 1947, is now more prosperous than it has been in two thousand years. The world, which was polarized explosively between East and West ten years ago, is returning to its normal order of confusion. The superpowers are relaxed.

Inhumanity goes on as ever, but the old nineteenth-century colonies are at last getting the chance to shape their own destinies.

Even the twentieth-century satellites are less bullied than under Stalin. In America car sales have rarely been higher, diet has never been fatter, housing has never been better and the Negro revolution eschews terror for the Constitution.

And yet it would be a rash man who suggested that this was peace. We are all too accustomed to hot, hyperthyroid thinking to recognize peace if it appears. Twenty-five years of racing to fires, dashing to stamp out bomb fuses and listening for spies in the cellar have created a spasm mentality. We need a constant supply of crises, races and challenges as an addict needs drugs.

No one thinks it at all odd that an attempt to do something decent for the jobless should be sloganized as "the war on poverty." That scientific study of the outer environment should be called "the race for space." That the attempt to spread democracy should be called "the battle for men's minds."

People who are conditioned to think of everything in terms of wars, battles, races and challenges eventually start con-

3

verting all experiences into struggles for survival. Life itself naturally becomes "the rat race." Adolescence becomes "the crisis of American youth."

Middle-age spread becomes a national challenge. Athletes are brought to the White House to warn that the flabby abdomen is the hidden ally of Communism.

Everyday living becomes a frantic succession of perils. The typical husband comes home from "the rat race" to find that a neighbor has moved ahead of him in "the struggle for status" by acquiring a new car or a power mower. His children, depending upon their age, are imperiled by "the school crisis," "the crisis of higher education," or "the marriage problem."

His wife has probably been "fighting traffic" somewhere in her struggle to solve "the leisure-time problem" and if the cleaning woman failed to show up, she may be bitter about "the woman's rights struggle."

People in this state of mind must be spoken to sharply if their attention is to be commanded. For this reason they are constantly being exhorted and shouted at. If their minds start to unwind, they are snapped briskly back to business by that dreary command, "Think," which hangs on the wall of every American's subconscious.

If there is a moment to doze by the television, it will be shattered by a one-two punch—first the crisis, then the command. For example: "There is another political uproar surrounding the White House tonight where President Johnson has again caught a beagle by the ear. We'll have that story right after this message. . . . Say, have you looked at your car's sludge-pump filter lately? Go to your friendly so-so station first thing tomorrow and have them show you what a clogged sludge-pump filter can do to your sludge consumption."

It is hard to see the world as it is when everyone is shouting and telling you that good citizenship compels you to look for doomsday at every bus stop. If it were not so hard to think at a slow amble, we might see that the shouters have confused plain, troublesome, old peace with dull, smug

4

nirvana, where everyone is fully insured against the accident of living.

As e. e. cummings once wrote to the un-alarmed: "You and I wear the dangerous looseness of doom and find it becoming. Life, for eternal us, is now; and now is much too busy being a little more than everything to seem anything, catastrophic included."

The late, late war

An insomniac's history of World War II, synthesized from fifteen years of watching TV at midnight:

Fortunately, when the Japanese bombed Pearl Harbor on December 7, 1941, Gary Cooper was at sea on the aircraft carrier Enterprise and, hence, survived to win the Battle of Midway, with Walter Brennan and Bruce Bennett fighting strong supporting roles.

The Japanese failure to time their attack so as to catch Cooper, Brennan and Bennett in drydock typified the ineptitude of the Axis powers. Neither Berlin nor Tokyo ever clearly saw the importance of destroying such vital elements of the Allied force as Errol Flynn, Humphrey Bogart, Gregory Peck, Cary Grant, Robert Taylor and James Cagney.

This miscalculation cost them dearly. By mid-1942, the Axis was up against the most awesome concentration of box-office power ever assembled. The only enemy who seems to have understood the hopelessness of his situation was Sir Cedric Hardwicke, to whom the Nazis assigned the impossible task of preventing Errol Flynn and Ann Sheridan from throwing the German Army out of Norway.

"It will do no good to hang them," Sir Cedric said at one point when his inferiors were preparing to execute a dozen supporting players in retaliation for the killing of Helmut Dantine. Sir Cedric, one of the most perceptive actors of the

5

war, knew that even though Dantine would return to fight another picture the Axis manpower situation was hopeless.

At the peak of Axis strength, the enemy's first-line forces were limited to Dantine, Eric Von Stroheim, Conrad Veidt, Abner Biberman and Philip Ahn. Ahn had been recruited from the *Charley Chan* family and Biberman was drafted from the supporting cast of "Gunga Din."

J. Carroll Naish, though serving under Mussolini, was a weak reed. Constantly explaining that he had relatives in the United States, he was always out of sympathy with the Nazis. In fact, Naish, more than any other actor, may have been responsible for the Axis' easy defeat through saving Bogart's life with water during the Sahara campaign.

Had Bogart not survived, Von Stroheim would have won the Battle of El Alamein. Moreover, without Bogart, the Allied powers would never have kept the North Atlantic route open to Murmansk, and the devastating roundup of Nazi spies in New York (which put Peter Lorre out of action) would never have been pulled off by Bogey's gangster pals.

Worst of all, Ingrid Bergman would probably have fallen in love at Casablanca with Claude Rains, who—hedonist that he was—would not have sent her to Lisbon with Paul Henreid, as Bogart did. It is difficult to believe that Henreid, without Ingrid Bergman at his side, could have masterminded the anti-Nazi resistance inside Europe.

Even with Bogart out of action, of course, the Axis would have had its hands full. Flynn, after liberating Norway, moved east and retook Burma from the Japanese in 90 minutes.

Cagney, having received the Medal of Honor for writing "Over There," had joined the O.S.S. and was undermining the German occupation of France. Pat O'Brien and Van Johnson had bombed Tokyo, wiping out Ahn and Biberman twice, while Cary Grant had taken his submarine into Tokyo Bay and torpedoed the Imperial Fleet.

While all this was going on, Brian Donlevy made the first atomic bomb. Thanks to Walter Pidgeon's rescue of the British Army at Dunkirk and Greer Garson's capture of Helmut Dantine, Britain had been secured as a base from which Van Johnson could lunge into Fortress Europa and win the Battle of the Bulge.

It is apparent today that the Axis had challenged an unconquerable force—a battalion of leading men who could never be wounded except inconsequentially in the shoulder and an audience that demanded happy endings for every battle.

Green elephant

One of the biggest rackets in the country today is grass. A statistician has figured that Americans spend $1.5 billion annually on their lawns, and this sum barely begins to express the toll that grass exacts from the society.

The number of man-hours and boy-hours that are wasted mowing, trimming, fertilizing, planting, currying and watering grass is incalculable. Men collapse of over-exertion in grass culture. Millions of hours are spent listening to grass bores. Respectable citizens are silently blackguarded by their neighbors for grass failure.

Hundreds of thousands of children are started down the road to neurosis by parents with grass anxiety. ("If I catch you playing on that grass once more, it's up to bed!") Valuable weekend sleeping time is destroyed by grass-proud neighbors running their power mowers through the morning dew.

And what does the country get for it all? Grass. There is nothing wrong with grass when taken in moderation. It nourishes the herbivorous beast, cools the concrete city and cushions tramps and lovers. The fact is, however, that we are letting grass get out of hand.

To begin with, we have perverted most of grass's natural

functions. A lawn is not grown to nourish the goat or cow. Any goats or cows that got onto it would be, like the children, sent immediately to bed. Tramps and lovers are hustled off it by the police. The grass must be respected.

As a result, most grass has become virtually useless and the grass around the typical American home has become a money-gobbling albatross, or, to switch metaphors, a green elephant.

The sensible way to build a house, as the Romans discovered two thousand years ago, is to put a blind wall up against the street line and face the living quarters onto a central court or yard. Instead, we set them back from the sidewalk and fill the wasted space with grass.

What purpose does the grass serve? It cannot be used to sustain a cow. The cow is certain to wander into the street and collide with an automobile. The family cannot picnic on it. It affords no privacy. For the same reason, it is useless for courting or sunbathing.

Although useless, it cannot be ignored, for a family is judged in its own neighborhood by the quality of its lawn. And so, the grass must be constantly beautified, fed, manicured, combed, caressed.

Grass is the least rewarding of all status symbols. The gleaming land cruiser parked in front of the grass may be ludicrously loaded with chrome, but at least it will move people around the country. The coach lamps on the portico may look pretentious, but at least they relieve the dark.

The grass does nothing but drink money, exhaust energies, crush spirits, destroy sleep, create tensions and interfere with the watching of baseball games, and sprout insolent signs ordering humans to keep off it.

Recently, there have been some evil developments in the grass racket. One such is the rise of the powered grass mower. Until a few years ago, it was sufficient to keep the grass cut. Then we came to a time when status depended on keeping it cut with a powered mower, one of the century's more dangerous machines, what with its ugly propensity for slicing off toes.

Now it is no longer enough simply to cut the grass, or to cut it with a power mower. It must be cut with a powered mower which can be operated from a driver's seat.

One of the oddities about the American's surrender to grass is his insistence that he likes it. Catch him perspiring in his useless Zoysia, and he will tell you, "Great exercise. Keeps me out in the sun." No use telling him that he could get the same results from tennis or lying on the beach, for he will come back with a cutting piece of grassmanship. ("Say, you've really let your clover get away from you, haven't you?")

The question we must all ask ourselves is, "When is this grass going to start earning its keep?"

A gallop in the edelweiss

Followers of the mass-circulation magazines may have noticed an important development. The monopolistic lock on magazine space once held by Jacqueline Kennedy and Elizabeth Taylor has been broken by a new feminine idol—New European Woman.

New European Woman is the wife of Western Europe's new boomtime millionaire. In fact, according to Cosmopolitan, which seems to have discovered her, she is the guiding purpose behind the Common Market. "Beautiful, sophisticated, wealthy woman," Cosmopolitan asserts, is "the end product of the burgeoning Common Market."

Hundreds of magazine layouts have been devoted to this astounding creature, and there are thousands more yet to come. All of them will look and sound just like this:

"Like an infinitely more slender Venus rising from the spume of Cytherea, Contessa Pepe y Pepe al-Peperino, archtype of stunningly feminine New European Woman, emerges

9

(left) from the sauna of her castle on the Aegean. Oils by Giotto and Cellini salt cellars are barely visible through the steam. 'Without art to lend proportion to the steam,' she says, 'the sauna is utterly lacking in ambiance.'

"Typifying the new young international sophisticates, the Contessa is as much an end product of booming Common Market Europe as the pig-iron freighting the ships of Ostend or the roaring beer busts held nightly in Heidelberg. Descended from a Ruthenian count and a long line of Argentine gauchos, the Contessa also traces collateral family roots to viziers of the Ottoman Empire.

"Her husband, who was rolling fettucini in Rome's Alfredo's in 1947, has ridden the economic boom well. Today he directs a syndicate with holdings in iron and steel, cars, machine tools, Middle East oil, New York real estate.

"To get more time with the luxurious Contessa, he commutes up to 800 miles a day, flying his own private plane, 'Horst Wessel,' from any of his nine castles to any of his dozens of plants.

"When not jetting off for weekends at Acapulco, Gstaad or their hideaway in the Orkneys, Contessa and Pepe like to relax informally on one of his yachts. 'True, I am equally at home in Caracas, San Francisco or Biarritz,' says the Contessa, 'but I am a simple girl. The crowds of Venice and the Cote d'Azur have always terrified me. I'm not really secure until Pepe and I are off in one of the yachts with the Titians and Picassos to soothe me and a few chic duchesses or royal emigres to talk horses with.'

"The Contessa, of course, is an enthusiastic horsewoman. Here (right) she wears chinchilla slacks and sweater woven entirely of ropes of pearls as she mounts her favorite stallion, Talleyrand, for a gallop in the edelweiss. Her interests also include ballet, action painting, sculpture, Lieder and charity.

" 'Life without charity,' she says, 'would be as empty as sauna without art.' The facility with which she coins such aphorisms has earned her the nickname 'Tete d'Oeuf.'

" 'But,' she insists, 'I'm not bright at all, actually. When-

10

ever we have people like Noel Coward or Bertrand Russell or Andre Malraux out to the castle for a weekend I can never think of anything really clever to say.'

"Above all, the Contessa is, par excellence, mother. At Christmas she took son Pumpsie-Boy, 6, for a mother-son holiday alone at Mont Fettucini, one of the family's three privately owned mountains in Switzerland, and taught him slalom racing. Next spring she plans to teach him scuba diving and has already leased the Arabian coast of the Red Sea to insure privacy for the lessons.

"Although the Common Market has produced hundreds of other women just as stunningly incredible as the Contessa, the arbiter of Common Market feminity, Princess Mona Lamonica de la Plage, insists that no previous civilization has seen a woman so nearly approaching the feminine ideal.

"But surely, it was suggested, the Princess overlooked American Woman, who had ruled supreme from 1945 until the birth of Gaullist Europe. 'Ah!' snorted the Princess. 'The American woman! I will tell you in truth, sir, that compared to the woman being produced today by the Common Market, the New World has not yet produced anything that could even be called Woman. I should except, perhaps, Madame Kennedy.' "

Teleball

No one took it seriously, of course, when the Columbia Broadcasting System, upon purchasing the New York Yankees, stated that network operations would not be permitted to become intertwined with the Yankee management.

On the other hand, no one quite foresaw how drastically network philosophy would ultimately change the nature of baseball. The reader will recall that shortly after C.B.S. bought the Yankees the National Broadcasting Company

11

snapped up the old New York Mets and the American Broadcasting Company bought the Los Angeles Dodgers.

Within two years the networks were locked in a murderous behind-the-scenes competition for baseball leadership, and all their resolve to keep hands off the game went by the wayside as vice presidents felt the pressure to raise attendance, or else.

The first big change for the C.B.S. Yankees occurred after the N.B.C. Mets had beaten them at the box office for the third consecutive year. The pre-eminence of the Mets showed unmistakably, C.B.S. announced, that what the public wanted was hillbilly baseball.

Accordingly, the announcement went on, C.B.S. planned to sign ten of the most ludicrous ball players in the country for the coming season and have Mr. Johnny Keane insert them in the line-up late in all games in which the Yankees had run up insuperable leads.

The policy was an instant success, and the A.B.C. Dodgers were able to hold their own only by packing their squad heavily with gangsters and cowboys, whose off-the-field antics kept a high level of viewer interest.

As the quality of baseball declined, intellectuals and long hairs protested that the game was being destroyed. Privately, network executives agreed. "Look," they told the intellectuals, "we appreciate good baseball as much as you do, but the slobs won't sit still for it. It is our duty to give the people what they want."

In no time at all, however, the Yankees were in fresh trouble. After losing the pennant three years in a row, C.B.S. was handed a bad scare when seven viewers of Italian-American extraction wrote letters charging the network with depicting Italian-Americans as baseball incompetents.

They referred to the casting of an Italian-American, Mr. Joe Pepitone, as first baseman on a losing team, and to the firing of Mr. Yogi Berra, with the suggestion that he had been responsible for the Yankees' defeat in 1964. By such actions, they charged, C.B.S. was insulting Italian-Americans everywhere.

12

C.B.S. promptly dropped Mr. Pepitone's contract and hired a new first baseman named Jones, who wasn't much of a ball player but was blessed with a nondescript face. The network reasoned that while retaining Mr. Pepitone would not hurt the box office, the corporation could not risk an Italian-American boycott of its soap and horse operas. Mr. Berra, who had found shelter with the N.B.C. Mets, was rehired by C.B.S., asked to change his name to Berramore and given a position as permanent panelist on "What's My Line?"

This crisis had scarcely blown over when the Daughters of the American Revolution denounced C.B.S. for having a left fielder on its payroll. In the ensuing Congressional investigation Mr. Tom Tresh admitted that he was the employe in question, but stated that he had drifted innocently into left field before anyone knew that television was going to take over baseball.

In a brilliant stroke C.B.S. persuaded N.B.C. and A.B.C. to join it in abolishing left field. It was a position, their joint statement said in which there was no mass viewer interest due to its remoteness from the cameras.

The revolution in the game occurred the following year when C.B.S. announced that the Yankees would discontinue live baseball and play exclusively on tape. This, the network explained, would enable C.B.S. to tape an entire six months' season in three months of concentrated winter play, thus cutting costs and permitting the networks to edit out long stretches of dullness which characterized so much live base-ball. Thereafter, they announced, the game would be called teleball.

N.B.C. quickly followed suit and topped C.B.S. by announcing that it had assigned Huntley and Brinkley to manage the Mets and narrate the tapes. In an effort to recover, C.B.S. announced that it was recalling Yogi Berramore from "What's My Line?" and teaming him with Walter Cronkite to battle N.B.C. in the ratings.

With General Eisenhower managing and narrating the taped A.B.C. Dodgers, teleball became the biggest TV game since "The $64,000 Question." The bubble finally burst when the producers were caught rigging the tapes, to stimulate viewer interest. Teleball has never recovered in this country, though in Japan one can still see the quaint old nine-inning, nine-man sport known as baseball.

The decline of sin

The first "billiard lounges" are just beginning to crop out of the landscape, but there is good reason to expect that they will soon cover the country. It is another troubling example of the American weakness for leaping before we look.

A "billiard lounge," of course, is basically a fumigated poolroom. The new race of "billiard lounge" operators is quite candid about it; their goal is to rehabilitate the American poolroom, to make it the kind of place a fellow would be proud to bring his girl to. Or even his mother.

The operators of Cushion & Cue, a new "billiard lounge" in Manhattan, advertise wall-to-wall carpeting, soft background music, air conditioning, check room, automatic food dispensers "set into a leisurelike snack area" and hostesses. "We sincerely hope," they add, "that we may also be instrumental in eventually eliminating the old 'poolrooms' and the stigma created by them from this most genteel game."

All this raises an important question that ought to be asked by the people who worry about national goals and purpose. Do we really want to do away with the old poolroom? If we do, what are we going to blame sin on?

Not so long ago this country was infested with a variety of iniquitous sinks where a young man could be quickly lured to ruin. Poolrooms, bowling alleys, saloons, drug store corners, horse parlors, roadside cabins—these were the main stops on the road to perdition, and every young man was on clear notice from the day he put on long pants that safety rested only in home and family.

14

Look at what's happened. The old bowling alleys have been rehabilitated and converted into wholesome family "recreation centers." The high school set has abandoned the drug store corner for the automobile, and everybody is now more worried about their driving than their morals.

As for the saloon, mother has long since barged in, installed wall-to-wall carpeting and dim lights, run up the price of beer and converted the place into the cocktail lounge. The horse parlor has been legalized and turned into the State of Nevada, where the whole family can be together around the one-armed bandit. The roadside cabins—nice people wouldn't even talk about them thirty years ago—are now luxury family hotels with wading pools for the kiddies.

In each case, the process has been the same. Family has invaded the precincts of sin with a big bank account, and the result has been a cleaning-up, a fumigating, a sweeping-out of the impecunious oafs and louts who were the old conventional sinners.

In these rehabilitated precincts of sin, success depends on creating a pleasant family atmosphere. And so the old sinks and sinful institutions are either disappearing or becoming sissified. All over the country, people eager to have a whack at Satan are confined to denunciations of poor old Henry Miller.

When the poolroom is transformed into the "billiard lounge" there will be one less institution to hold accountable for the persistence of evil. Is it really a good idea to let it go down?

The question is silly, of course. If the American family cottons to "billiard lounges" as it did to the bowling alleys, the poolroom is done for, and there is no committee in Washington that can save it.

What is disturbing is the way truth has gone flexible on the sin issue. Now, with the Freudians rampant, every young man is notified that the source of sin is not the poolroom at all, but home and family. Good-by, harmless poolroom; hail, "billiard lounge," where a fellow would be proud to bring his girl. Or even his mother.

Lascivious eyes crinkled hungrily

From some future best seller's Washington novel, here is a page of manuscript left on the bus to Capitol Hill:

"The President's wasted hand trembled violently as he fought to compose himself for this final confrontation. 'Steady, Prez,' he told himself. 'Got·to be steady for this one, Prez.'

"But when he thought again of the treachery of it his body surrendered to a shudder of revulsion. To think that Astrohazy, his own Secretary of State, should be coming here to the White House to demand the surrender of the United States to the Kremlin. It was incredible. He could still not bring himself to accept it. But there was the evidence. Cold, brutal, irrefutable: his own Secretary of State was none other than the mysterious Comrade Ubiquitov, known only to Central Intelligence as 'Number Three in the Politburo.'

"The President's secretary cut across his train of thought. 'Cal Simpkins is here, Mr. President,' she said. She wanted to weep when she saw his ruined face. He's dying, she thought. How can they do this to him? 'Send him in,' said the President wearily.

"He despised Simpkins but knew that of all the Senators on Capitol Hill none would make a more reliable partner in the awful ordeal that lay ahead. Simpkins, he realized, might be a thief, a lecher and a boor, but no other man in Congress loved America more or would fight more fiercely to keep her from going down.

"Simpkins strode into the office with his customary ruthless gait, the familiar cunning smile painted on his handsome solon's face.

" 'Cal,' said the President, 'we've never exactly loved one another.'

"Simpkins let his handsomely insincere features express a

16

noncommittal benign evil. 'There's been bad news, Cal,' the President continued.

" 'I know,' Simpkins said. 'The Chinese Reds have just landed the first death-ray crew on Mars and are threatening to disintegrate Milwaukee Tuesday morning unless we turn NATO over to them. I read it on the ticker just before I left the Capitol.'

" 'No, Cal. I mean really bad news.'

" 'Don't let that worry you, Mr. President. We know the Chairman of the Atomic Energy Commission didn't really die of a fall in the bathtub last week. The word has a way of getting around on the Hill. We knew all along that he'd been threatening to blow up New York unless you agreed to a sneak nuclear attack on Moscow. Some of us kind of admire the way you handled that one, Mr. President.'

" 'Cal,' the President murmured feebly, glaring at Simpkins with steely obsolescent eyes, 'thank God you have the vision to see America clearly.'

" 'Afraid some of us are going to have to make a little noise about the way you had El Paso blown up without any warning last Monday,' Simpkins said.

" 'Yes, yes,' the President said tiredly. 'I know, but there was no alternative. One of our pilots went berserk and blew up Smolensk and we just had to give it to El Paso to keep the Russians from getting edgy.' The telephone jangled. 'Secretary Astrohazy is here,' said his secretary's voice. Before the line had clicked dead, the office door burst open.

"A glance told the President that his Secret Service bodyguard had been gassed. What stunned him even more was the identity of the woman standing at Astrohazy's side, gas gun in hand. 'Belle Traymore, the arbiter of Washington society!' he gasped.

"Astrohazy uttered a throaty chuckle of gloating and Belle's lascivious eyes crinkled as they hungrily embraced Simpkins with glances darting fire."

Here the manuscript page ends. Will the author please claim it?

Everything, absolutely everything

This must be the only country in history that spends the entire month of December every year worrying how to do more for The Man Who Has Everything.

"Of course, it's only fitting," The Man Who Has Everything said recently over an expense-account mousse flambé, "considering that it spends the other eleven months deploring handouts to the man who has nothing."

He was expansive, having just finished a superb duck galatine which would be financed by the Treasury as a deductible business cost, and over an Uppmann and brandy he dilated upon the difficulties of his life.

"Too many people think it's a soft touch having everything," he said. "They don't know what it means to be harassed every December to think of something new that will make you happy."

In desperation he has frequently suggested gifts like a hand-carved ivory abacus or an electronic garage-door opener, which have severely complicated his life. As a learning exercise on the abacus, he once started to compute his outstanding credit card bills and ended up in psychoanalysis.

After installing his electronic garage-door opener he discovered that his garage door was opening mysteriously during the night when the gadget was out of use. After several weeks the mystery was solved. A neighbor had acquired an electronic martini muddler which regularly became confused and opened the garage door when it should have been muddling gin.

"You wouldn't believe the things I have," he went on. "An ice bowl shaped like a bowling ball. A bowling ball colored like an ice bowl. A pet monkey, an executive foot massager, an executive personal plug-in sun-tanner, a Civil War chess set, a wax Easter egg with a carved wax bunny inside, coconut-husk suspenders, a chinchilla cummerbund, a mink woodpile cover, a year's lessons in flamenco dancing, the executive picture book of the great ideas of Western man. . . ."

The Man Who Has Everything has not always had everything. He can recall, as a boy, taking his wagon to the relief center to get his family's ration of corn meal, prunes and tinned grapefruit juice. "Those were terrible days," he reflected.

"In those days everybody still needed things. I wanted some real tinned pineapple juice instead of that awful grapefruit juice, and I wanted a new wagon so I wouldn't look so shabby when I went in to collect the corn meal. I wanted them so badly that I needed them."

What was the secret of his rise to Everything? "I saw very clearly one day that the secret was to want things you didn't need. After I moved up to pineapple juice, I wanted papaya juice. After I got a new wagon I wanted a bicycle, and then later, a car, and then a car with white sidewalls."

In no time he had found the key to everything. He saw that an economy that produced only what he needed would never get him off corn meal in a cold-water flat. The way to the great restaurants was to make the economy to swamp him in things he didn't need.

Now, at the pinnacle, he sometimes lies awake, haunted by the fear that some day he will wake up with nothing needless to want. On that day, he believes, the bubble will burst and all the credit-card collectors will arrive at the door en masse.

After nights like this, he rises and tells his wife, "All right, I'll keep the gold lawn mover. The neighbors will hate me, but somebody has to save them from tinned grapefruit juice and corn meal."

Goodbye, hubcaps

Here is a typical middle-of-the-night civics problem of the sort that makes the nineteen-sixties a constant headache:

It is ten minutes before three o'clock in the morning and downstairs at the curb in front of the house a well-dressed young man is noisily removing your hubcaps. The noise has wakened you to a state of semiconsciousness and, groggy with sleep, you stagger to the window and watch him work.

Your first rational thought is, "Why does it have to be my hubcaps?" The city is full of hubcaps, many of them of surpassing brilliance. The young man obviously does not need just any old hubcaps, for his own car, parked alongside yours in the middle of the street, is a yellow convertible of the latest vintage.

At its wheel sits another young man—the getaway driver. These young men's parents have obviously been good to them because you don't buy yellow convertibles of the latest vintage with the proceeds from hot hubcaps.

In any case, the first sleepy emotion is a bitter surge of self-pity. "If my parents had bought me a yellow convertible when I was sixteen," you think, "I wouldn't have driven it around stealing working men's hubcaps." As the brain comes alert, however, the necessity for taking responsible civic action asserts itself.

One recalls the Genovese case in New York, in which thirty-eight citizens woke in the night and did nothing while hearing a woman being murdered. What is the citizen's duty when witnessing his hubcaps being stolen?

As the citizen involved in this case tells it, he immediately canvassed a number of alternatives. The first was to put on his robe, go outside and confront the young man. This he rejected because:

(1). He had forgotten where he put his robe. (2). He

20

feared that the young man might open his skull with the tire iron he was using on the hubcaps. (3). He has always had a foppish distaste for having curious crowds clustered around him while lying unconscious and bleeding on the sidewalk, in his pajamas.

The second alternative was to point a gun out the window and order the young man to reach for the sky, or better yet, to fire two warning shots through his windshield. Unfortunately or not, he had no gun. He had reasoned years ago that men who keep guns in their bedrooms commonly end up shot by their wives. Long ago, in the sane waking hours, he had decided that it would be better to lose a few hubcaps in life than to give a nervous woman access to live ammunition.

Alternative number three was to bluff; that is, to pretend that he had a gun and shout out the window, "Stand right where you are until the police arrive, or I'll shoot." This he knew he could not do without sounding ridiculous.

The fourth alternative was to telephone to police. This he also rejected. He reasoned as follows: If the police failed to arrive in time, he would spend the rest of his night filling out police reports.

If the police did arrive in time to save the hubcaps, endless difficulties would surely ensue. He would have to appear in court as prosecutor of the young men. Having a yellow convertible, they would doubtless have superb lawyers who might persuade a jury that any man who leaves hubcaps on the street at 3 A.M. should be charged with corrupting youth.

Moreover, there would be terrible courtroom confrontations with the youths' parents. ("How can you do this to our sons for a set of common hubcaps?") Moreover, the court might very possibly rule that these boys were merely expressing their hostility to a society that gives them too many yellow convertibles, and might turn them loose to come back and slash the tires next time a hostile society cut their beer off at 2 A.M.

What the witness to the crime actually did was yell out the

21

window, "Hey, put those hubcaps back!" The young men sped away carrying the hubcaps and the witness went back to sleep after fifteen minutes of hating himself.

He is an indulgent father. In time he will make all his children love him by buying them yellow convertibles.

Cyrano de IBM-709

A young man in Florida has taught a computer to write poetry. He feeds the machine seventy-eight words, including twenty simple phrases, sets it to use noun, adjective, verb in orderly sequence, and the machine grinds out thirty poems a minute.

Here is a sample:

> *Darkly the peaceful trees crash*
> *In the serene sun*
> *While the heart heard*
> *The swift moon stopped silently.*

The author of these lines is IBM-709. Capable of only forty-two thousand mathematical additions per second, it is considered obsolete among modern computers, which may account for the brooding tone of some of its best lines. (For example: "The darkly reality grew harshly"; "Fearfully the silent fields faded"; "The heavy landscape crashed suddenly.")

Nevertheless, obsolete or not, IBM-709 will eventually be able to turn out five hundred poems a minute, according to forecasts from Tallahassee. The pity is that there is no practical use for this talent. Poetry nowadays sells little better than horse collars, and any poet who cannot fortify his income with a curmudgeon act or lecture-circuit jokes is hard put to pay the milkman.

IBM-709 can expect nothing but contempt from his fellow

22

computers. It is painful to imagine him turning up at class reunions and computer conventions. "That's old 709," the high-speed boys will whisper, "he's down to writing poetry."

At the bar, running tetrameter through his tubes, he will be hounded with subtle sneering questions, "How many poets have you put out of work this year, 709?"

And, "Why don't you come up to Washington this fall and help us call the election six minutes before the polls close?"

Being a poet has its compensations, however, and in time 709 will discover them. One of these is that most ladies, or at least most ladies whom a computer would want to spend an evening with, would far rather have a poem than a red-hot election statistic.

Once 709 starts turning out five hundred poems a minute —seven hundred twenty thousand poems every twenty-four hour day—this fact about women is going to occur to some handsome, inarticulate computer genius and he is going to bear one of 709's better sonnets to his unattainable Roxanne.

Everybody knows Roxanne. Nothing leaves her colder than Christian's small talk about binary numerals and circuit telemetry. But let him arrive one night with a 709 sonnet about the swift moon stopping suddenly and she will show him a moon that the N.A.S.A. computing center has never dreamed of.

The trouble, of course, as everyone knows who has read "Cyrano de Bergerac," is that sooner or later Roxanne will learn that her Christian is only a mutterer about binary numerals and that the poet she truly loves is old IBM-709.

Tragedy? Not for 709. He is only a machine, after all. It is an easy matter to take his vocabulary out of his tubes and reduce him once more to a mere calculator.

For Roxanne the psychic damage is not so easily repaired. It is a hard thing for a woman to discover that she is really in love with a machine. It doesn't help for Christian to tell her that the words were his, and that the machine merely arranged them in infinite combinations to make poetry. Every-

23

one can buy a dictionary; only a poet can rearrange it into music.

Computers that write poetry, music and novels, all doubtless inevitable, will be only tools to make Christian's life wealthier. But when they win the poetry award, applause at Lincoln Center and the Pulitzer Prize, Christian must also live with the knowledge that it is the machines, not he, that bewitch the world's Roxannes.

Man, his loneliness and why he deserves it

The possibility that dolphins may be trying to communicate with us is no laughing matter for the dolphins.

Dr. John Lilly, head of the Communication Research Institute, reports in Science, Journal of the American Association for the Advancement of Science, that captive dolphins in his laboratory are able to modify their normal vocal behavior —whistles, barks, grunts, creaking and rasping sounds—as if trying to speak with their human captors.

Indeed, one dolphin named Elvar is said to have reached the stage where he can utter something that sounds like "All right, let's go," when the researchers exhaust his patience. It is not an unreasonable sound to start with if the dolphins are going to start dealings with the human race, but it suggests an unwillingness to suffer fools which may also get them into trouble.

We mechanized mammals do not like being talked back to by marine life. There is a tacit assumption among the gentlest of us that we are in charge on this planet. If the dolphins mean to challenge it, they are in for an ugly awakening.

In fact, it is all too easy to foresee what would happen if Elvar should swim into his tank one day, grin up at Dr. Lilly and creak, rasp, bark or whistle, "Take me to your leader." Instead of getting an interview with Lyndon Johnson, he would wind up on the Ed Sullivan show, be impounded by the C.I.A. and held incommunicado until he revealed the apparatus and intentions of dolphin society.

It seems not unreasonable to believe that the dolphins have developed a happy accommodation with life on earth which may even be superior to the present stage of human society ("civilization"). The dolphin's brain appears to be not only as complex as man's, but also some 20 to 40 per cent larger; both factors are believed to bear on intelligence.

The difficult question is, why should they want to communicate with us? It has always been apparent to the world of beasts that communication is the root of most troubles in human society. The apes, whose human gestures strike such responsive chords in our primordial senses, have paid dearly.

The best an ape can hope for is a shabby career of scrambling for dimes from an accordion tether. Dogs, who for some reason strike man as sympathetic to the human condition, are treated almost as badly. You see them roped mercilessly to possessive ladies, being hauled off wretchedly to shampoo parlors or imprisonment in studio flats, or being slapped and belted into Prussian discipline of their tails.

Cats have handled the humans much more shrewdly. They refuse to make the slightest concession to human communication, and in consequence they get away with murder. Kicks, starvation and even threats of drowning leave the cats impervious to human tyranny.

Neither love nor hate can force them to try communicating, for the cats know that when a man starts thinking he can talk to you he will eventually make intolerable demands and reward you with miserable shampoos or cage you under a barrage of peanuts.

What the cats know, and what the dogs and apes have been too dense to grasp, is that the more a man is communicated with, the more difficult he becomes to live with.

When a letter took six months to arrive and most people couldn't even write, human society was in bad shape. Now when everybody can tell everybody else his troubles and when an ultimatum can be delivered in thirty seconds, human society is simply intolerable.

So far we have learned very little about the dolphins. We don't know if they are smarter than we, better organized, morally superior or better adjusted socially. If so, they may feel that they have something vital to tell us.

This would be a serious mistake for the dolphins, somewhat like flaunting a mink coat before the tax collector. If they are half as smart as they seem to be, they will keep their spout holes buttoned.

III

The Culture Explosion

The Philistine shortage

It was a shock to run into Buck Jim Von Clausenworthy wearing shoes and no beard. Over a martini and cigarettes— in the old days it had always been muscatel and "pot"—he explained that he had given up the active practice of art and, with it, the beard, the scrofulous turtleneck and the verminous jeans of his creative period.

He was a changed man from the triumphant Von Clausenworthy whose culminating masterpiece, "Derelict on Blue Radiator"—a live derelict sitting on a blue radiator—had electrified the art world in 1961.

"Derelict," he said, had sold for $32,000 to a Manhattan investment banker, who had moved it from his home to his office lobby after the first few times the derelict insisted on getting off the radiator and mingling with the guests at cocktails.

Von Clausenworthy smiled bitterly at the memory. "Derelict," he said, "convinced me that desperate measures were needed to save the American artist. I wanted to be denounced, attacked, spat on by the Philistines for perpetrating this farce. What happened? They made me a rich man."

At this point, Von Clausenworthy said, he saw for the first time that the modern artist was being destroyed by the lack of a hostile, bourgeois, narrow-minded audience. "For a while," he said, "I tried everything I could think of to get the Philistines to attack me, so that I could feel alienated as an artist should."

In this period he produced his celebrated "Rusty Shovel," a rusty shovel he had found in his garage rafters, and "Cerise Paint Tracks," a perceptive and tragic canvas executed by dipping his feet in ten-gallon cans of cerise paint, then dancing the watusi on a bedsheet. Nothing failed. The Philistines refused to rise.

29

"I finally saw the truth," Von Clausenworthy said. "There were no Philistines left; it was a terrible situation. Here we were, all of us artists, desperately needing Philistines to hate our work, and there were no Philistines left to help us. Art was being tolerated to death."

Von Clausenworthy decided that radical action was necessary to restore the artist's ancient sense of alienation from society. He abandoned art practice, shaved, dressed like a bourgeois, moved to Washington and set up a new lobby which does business under the name "Philistinism Now, Inc."

The object is to rally hostility against modern art. "It's hard work," he said. "Nobody wants to be a Philistine any more. They'd rather pay $20,000 for a rusty shovel than admit it doesn't say anything to them."

Von Clausenworthy's first project was an effort to make Allen Ginsberg, the poet, feel more out of the social mainstream. Ginsberg had appeared on a TV discussion panel and announced that he was going to say something that the television Philistines would censor off the tape.

He then said that he wanted to go home and smoke some "pot" (marijuana). The producer refused to censor it. "How do you think it makes Ginsberg feel to discover that he can't even be censored on television?" Von Clausenworthy asked. "I'm trying to save Ginsberg from feeling that he's square enough for television by getting up an angry-letter campaign against the producer."

Von Clausenworthy's second project was an effort to save a young artist named Lucas Samaras. Samaras had held a show at a Manhattan gallery, which included a replica of the cluttered 6x12 bedroom he occupied in New Jersey for fourteen years. It was simply a small cluttered room. "I see it as assemblage, even sculpture," Samaras told a reporter. His asking price: $17,000.

Hoping to bring Samaras the restorative sense of alienation, Von Clausenworthy tried to make a mockery of him by urging home-owners all over the East Coast to send their basement clutter intact to Manhattan art dealers for display as assemblage or sculpture.

He had very little luck. Most people, he discovered, upon learning that their cellar clutter is an "assemblage" or sculpture, would rather lose the sale price than admit it doesn't mean anything to them.

On with the mindlessness

A televiewer named Finney asks rather heatedly just what the television industry thinks it is up to.

This Finney bought his first TV set two years ago and had lived happily with it until recently when, sitting in front of the thing as usual one night, he felt a mild irritation between the ears. Upon checking, he discovered to his annoyance that he was thinking.

Investigation showed that he was thinking about the TV show he was staring at. In a few more minutes he was not merely thinking about it but deeply engaged in the problem on the screen, which concerned a recognizable human being in a recognizable human dilemma.

The show, called "The Defenders," left Finney so ruffled that he turned the set off, took two tranquilizers and went to bed early. During the next four weeks he had two other equally bad experiences—one with a show called "The Doctors and the Nurses" and the other with "Slattery's People."

"They're trying to destroy television," he says. His complaint is well taken, and the television industry will be wise to examine its responsibilities to the public before this thinking trend gets out of hand. If it lets theatrical pretension interfere with its duty to provide betel nut for the eyes, a lot of us are going to start looking elsewhere for our lethargy.

The charm of television entertainment is its ability to

31

bridge the chasm between dinner and bedtime without mental distraction. It is peace of mind in a box.

You leave the family problems at the dinner table, aim the eyes at the box and feel the mind slowly ease to the curb and stop. A pleasant slackness releases the jaw, the head droops gently and the body becomes soft and spongy under recurrent waves of dishwater, beer and gentle easy-on-the-brain soapsuds.

The older TV critics keep harking back to "the golden age" when television, they say, was Theater in the Living Room. This must have been terrible. Most theater nowadays is bad enough in the theater, where you can face it in a necktie and a clean shirt.

Surely nobody wants to have to sit in his living room in stocking feet and undershirt and have a box try to convince him that life is just a filthy trick. What television has given us is an easy way to get life off our minds. As the complainant Finney points out, "All I want from my box is a little uninterrupted coma."

There are times when some people want to rack their brains about what "Tiny Alice" or Ingmar Bergman really means. The proper places for this activity are the theater and movie house, and not the living room, where a man only wants to forget what Lyndon Johnson and Charles de Gaulle really mean, and what his wife really means, and what his boss really means, and what his doctor and broker and all those other nuisances really mean.

When a man lights up his box, he expects release; not escape, but release. When some amiable imbecile in a military uniform gambols across the glass, the viewer doesn't escape into the box's world. He merely stares at it with no sense of engagement and no thought of escape because the box's world is so remote from life that only another imbecile could possibly become involved.

The beauty of the thing is its refusal to put claims on the brain. It is to be stared at like the hypnotist's spinning watch. Pomaded cowboys, cardboard surgeons, women with bad breath, dreamboat detectives—they all flash by in pleasant kaleidoscopic confusion to release the mind from life.

Television entertainment has nothing to be ashamed of. It should realize, however, that its public duty is to keep us staring, and not to make us blink.

Ah ha, Carlo Ponti!

"The Conjugal Bed" is an Italian movie that has had a moderate success in this country, although it is difficult to see why. It is not hilariously funny, as the ads claim, and the salacious content which is supposed to distinguish all films of Mediterranean vintage is well below what a seasoned movie-goer expects of a low-budget California Bible epic.

As a documentary on life in the olive-oil belt of new, prospering Common Market Europe, however, it offers a good deal of psychological comfort to the American. For years, Europeans have been passing condescending judgments on the quality of American life as mirrored in Hollywood movies, and films like "The Conjugal Bed" give us all an opportunity to return the sneer.

Such self-indulgence would have been in bad taste before Europe recovered its economic and spiritual independence; one responsibility of great power is the duty to abide in silence the slanging of the less fortunate. Since Europe now insists, however, that it has returned to full superiority, it must also expect to be patronized. Two can play at the de Gaulle game.

The fact is that if Italy is to be judged on the testimony of its recent movies, it is a sick and dispirited land in which materialism rides roughshod over spiritual and cultural values and human relations are little better than bestial.

The theme of "The Conjugal Bed" is a cynical belittling of marriage. In crude allegory, the relation between husband

33

and wife is likened to the mating process between spiders. The difference is that the male spider, if quick on his feet, occasionally escapes with his life; the moral of "The Conjugal Bed" is that the man who yields to the clutches of marriage is inexorably doomed.

The same anti-human attitude suffuses "Divorce—Italian Style." In this, the wretched male, who is being slowly consumed by his spider wife, solves his problem by murder, and the community applauds him. What has material prosperity done to the race of Leonardo, Michelangelo and Rossellini?

Perhaps the most telling indictments of the new Italy are the incidental scenes which reveal how the new Italians live. They show a people in thrall to luxury gadgets, racy cars and soft living. The heroes lie in bed watching television and take their fruit juice out of blenders ("The Conjugal Bed"), spend hours oiling their coiffures ("Divorce—Italian Style"), and play pat-the-knee with unutterably beautiful women in luxury castles ("La Dolce Vita").

When someone goes to church, it is either comic or lewd. People rich enough to have visited Italy and to have met Italians on their own ground say that they aren't like this at all and that the movies misrepresent them. Perhaps so.

If they expect to continue cleaning up in the American film market, however, the Italians will have to take their lumps. It is a matter of simple justice. All those years when Americans had to defend themselves against European imputations that this was a country as uncouth as Edward G. Robinson and as sybaritic as Rita Hayworth have to be paid for.

The Italians are singled out here only because their films are Europe's least dismaying. France, as every patron of the art theaters knows, is rampant with gangsterism, casual brutality and the most cynical immorality, and Paris comes off the screen as the new Chicago.

And England, poor England, with all those nits and quacks and confidence men, is establishing itself as a human zoo. Sweden is a mental asylum, full of fog and hyperthyroid blondes baying at the moon. "Never on Sunday" and

"Phaedra" have revealed the Greeks. They live in a perpetual euphoria, idolize prostitutes and while away the Attic hours driving maniacally in sports cars, munching grapes in their villas and entertaining aboard their yachts. It is perversely satisfying to go to the movies and see all the evidence of European barbarity and cultural impoverishment.

There is no point in Europeans saying, "But we really don't live like that at all." A responsibility of great power, they must learn, is the duty to pocket your box-office receipts without an unseemly snarl of "sour grapes."

Use what *influence?*

Well, Zero Mostel opened in Washington in a new play and the critics said it was great and right away the tickets all disappeared from the box office of the National Theater.

It was obviously a waste of time to go down there and ask for three in the orchestra because everybody knows that within ten minutes after the critics say a play is great the box office will be occupied by a persnickety lady sitting there opening envelopes and telling you that the only thing left is standing room.

Sure enough, there she was, slitting envelopes. Sure enough, the only thing on sale at the box office was standing room. Somebody should do a treatise on the role of the box office in American life.

The research should also embrace the headwaiter and the hotel room clerk. The box office never has tickets, the headwaiter never has a table, and the room clerk never has a room. Oh, there are exceptions. The box office can turn up two on the aisle for a well-panned retread of "The Desert Song," and the room clerk can occasionally put you next door to the elevator.

In any case, the National's box office was bare. The

35

woman who wanted to see Zero said, "Use your influence." She wasn't even a very sophisticated woman, which shows how bad the ticket situation is getting to be. Ten years ago, most people would have taken the box office's word for it when told that there were no seats left.

Nowadays even unsophisticated females know better. What actually happens is this: When there is a successful play or a big game—like the World Series or a New York Giants football game—all the tickets leave the box office and go to a place to which only people with influence are admitted.

Money is not enough to possess these tickets; the buyer must establish that he is important enough to deserve them. Now comes the hard part, a time of testing that can leave a man scarred for days afterwards. He can phone the management and submit his credentials, which can be pretty humiliating if he is, say, J. J. Spivis, feed salesman of Steamboat Springs, Colo., member of the Diner's Club and valedictorian of his high school class.

His other options, which are even worse, are to test his influence with a business acquaintance in the armaments lobby, or to ask a bell captain to refer him to a good scalper. Both are bad choices. One tips off the lobbyist that Spivis lacks the influence to get tickets through a Senator, which hurts his business status, and if the bell captain won't help, Spivis probably goes back home crushed by the knowledge that he hasn't even enough influence to sway flunkeys.

What's worse, failure means that he has to go back to the woman who ordered him to "Use your influence" and admit that he doesn't have any. Men have been divorced for less. Everybody knows of two or three marriages that ended after husbands failed to qualify for tickets to "My Fair Lady."

There is a way out of the ticket nightmare. Influence ratings. An organization similar to Dun & Bradstreet would assign influence ratings to everybody who fancies himself anybody. A rating of 1 would go to the President, his Cabinet, Senators, industrialists who serve on advisory committees in political campaigns, people who have made the cover of Time, Bobby Baker, prominent television emcees, "names" like Zsa Zsa Gabor, Toots Shor, Stanislas Radziwill.

The hierarchy might extend down to a 10 rating, which would take in relief pitchers on pennant contenders, failed politicians like Carmine De Sapio, last year's Miss America, etc. Notices for a hit show, a World Series, a Giants game would then specify who was eligible for tickets. "This show for number 1 to 4 influence only," or "Sorry, influence ratings 8, 9 and 10, but bleacher tickets only are available for today's game."

It's a pipe dream, of course. The reality is hearing her ask, "Did you get tickets to Zero Mostel?" and answering, "No," and her asking, "Didn't you use your influence?" and answering, "I was afraid I'd find out that I don't have any."

The invisible artists

The film of "My Fair Lady" illustrates another paradox of the triumph of technology. It is giving us more and more to cheer but making it harder and harder to know what we are cheering for.

In the movie, Eliza Doolittle is spoken by Audrey Hepburn, but when Miss Hepburn parts her lovely lips to sing, the voice that emerges is the voice of a singer named Marni Nixon. This is called dubbing. The film is widely applauded.

The question that comes to mind is, what are the critics applauding for? Miss Hepburn's luminous camera presence, or Miss Nixon's way with a song? Neither, surely. It makes no sense to sit through a musical cheering a leading lady who is not singing and a singer who is invisible.

The answer is that the applause belongs to the technicians who have merged Miss Nixon's voice and Miss Hepburn's gestures into a single performance. Dubbing technology has reached a stage where it can manufacture complete artists

37

out of bits and pieces. Soon we will doubtless see Hamlet gesticulated by Rock Hudson in the voice of Sir John Gielgud and, someday perhaps, have Lyndon Johnson address us in the voice of Richard Burton.

There is something unsound here. It arises from public clamor for superhuman excellence in its performers. Julie Andrews, who both spoke and sang Eliza on Broadway, was rejected for the film on grounds that we will pay more to see a box-office "name" like Miss Hepburn, even though she has to sing in a rented soprano.

Synthetics of this sort are not new in films. They are as old as Bing Crosby's toupee and Gary Cooper's stunt man. In those days, however, technical synthetics were merely crutches to help the act along. Nowadays they are becoming the act.

Teen-age crooning is a case. Even our daughters who swoon over these furred "idols" are smart enough to know that they can't sing "Dardanella" in the bathtub without their echo chambers and tape splicers.

Situation comedy on television has thrived for years on "canned" laughter grafted to gaglines by technicians using records of guffawing audiences that have been dead for years. But technology's takeover is not confined to entertainment. It has completely destroyed what used to be called football.

Football is no longer a sport for contending "elevens"—a headline word that has passed out of use—but a scientifically orchestrated mass beef ballet. The coach is now a master football technician with a staff of specialists.

Their goal is perfection. For this purpose they command exquisitely trained platoons of specialists who shuttle on and off field to insure that each play will be executed by the most specialized experts available.

It is magnificent, but it isn't football; it's a competitive exhibition in football technology between two mammoth organizations. And what are the crowds applauding—the vast "teams" which run up to sixty experts at some colleges, or the technological skill of the coaches who fuse dozens of specialized talents into a graceful display of football arts?

Politics is another problem. The lips were the lips of Barry Goldwater, but the words were the words of Karl Hess, his ghostwriter. Were we howling for Goldwater, or for Hess? For President Johnson, or for one of his cadre of spooks?

It may be that we don't care much, as long as the need to howl, cheer, swoon, laugh and applaud is gratified. This demand has become more than normal human performers can satisfy. We want box-office smash and glorious soprano in a single film, two swoons a week from the juke box, thirty laughs a night from television, sixty gridiron thrills every weekend and ten speeches a day from politicians.

Individual human capacity to keep our cravings down is exhausted, which may explain why we now need the technologists to keep us titillated with synthetic superhumans. And what we applaud is often no longer individual excellence, but the ingenuity with which our technicians deceive us. No wonder we have become the world's greatest consumers of wax bananas and plastic roses.

Modernized library

Mortimer Adler, the Great Books man, confesses in Playboy that some of the classics bore even him. If Dr. Adler can't stand Cicero, it seems reasonable to assume that we Playboy-oriented masses find the going just as tough with the lighter classics which we have been avoiding since high school.

The problem, for a nation self-consciously aware that it is supposed to be undergoing a cultural explosion, is how to keep the classics alive. The solution would seem to lie in bringing them up to date, possibly by commissioning the foremost writers of the day to rework them in terms that are meaningful to culturally exploding moderns.

To illustrate what can be done, here is a hypothetical pub-

39

lisher's list of a book house that might be called Modernized Library:

ANNA KARENINA by Henry Miller. In his revivification of Tolstoy's lugubrious Tsarist soap opera, Miller, writing in the first person through Vronsky's eyes, shifts the scene from Russia to Paris of the 1930's to illuminate the mystical hedonism of a profligate young Count fleeing American materialism. In his liaison with Anna, the half-wit wife of a French telegraph deliveryman, Vronsky perceives that the essential evil of woman is her destructive hatred of man's polygamous nature. With characteristic exhaustiveness, Miller finally answers all questions about what went on in the bedroom between Anna and Vronsky in some of the most explicit prose ever published by Modernized Library.

HEIDI by Terry Southern and Mason Hoffenberg. A scathingly existentialist satire on the morality of Swiss peasantry living at the foot of Europe's most fashionable ski runs. Nothing like it since Vladimir Nabokov's "Little Women." Banned in Paris.

HUCKLEBERRY FINN by James Baldwin. This long awaited indictment of the white liberal is at once a tender and infuriated cry from the heart. Jim, its protagonist, is ostensibly aided by the typical well-meaning but shallow white liberal, Huck, in his flight from the sinister Miss Watson. As the two drift down the Mississippi, the pent-up hatred on their raft gradually builds to the breaking point, a moment of fury in which Jim makes Huck understand that he is bigoted because he, like Miss Watson, is incapable of love. In despair, Jim leaps to his death from the raft. Huck sails on to what will clearly be the sterile lifetime of a hack writer sending small sums anonymously to Jim's sister as conscience balm.

THE ADVENTURES OF SHERLOCK HOLMES by William S. Burroughs. Holmes, a cocaine addict, is seen on the opening page snatching a bowler in the Charing Cross underground station to get pawnshop money for his pusher. We then follow him, more or less, on a bizarre romp through London, always one step ahead of Scotland Yard. Holmes's cocaine hallucinations—of everything from murderous hounds to nude hanging scenes involving his junkie pal, Dr. Watson—

constitute the most pungent statement ever composed against law enforcement.

A Tale of Two Cities by Joseph Heller. Sydney Carton, the only sane man in the world at the close of the eighteenth century, sees quite clearly that the French revolution is a racket. His uproarious attempts to win Charles Darnay's wife, without having his head cut off, end in a comic riot when his scheme to send Darnay to the guillotine backfires and Mrs. Darnay, instead, winds up in the tumbril. Carton's decision not to take her place under the blade is insanely logical.

Wuthering Heights by Tennessee Williams. Heathcliff, a brooding delicate lad who has been psychically mutilated by his domineering mother, is marked for marriage by the lusty, possessive Cathy, and the stage is set for tragedy. Williams provides it when Heathcliff falls into a pen of half-starved hogs. The critics will argue for years whether Heathcliff's fall was an act of will.

The Iliad by Norman Mailer. Set in Los Angeles, Mailer's "Iliad" begins when Paris, who has just murdered his wife and is trying to savor the existential essence of the deed, meets the Hollywood sex goddess, Helen, in a nightclub and wins her away from her producer, Menelaus, by doing the best rumba in the house. "I could smell the hate on Menelaus thick as sink grease," says Paris, as he squires Helen off to a Palm Springs weekend of blood, nausea and strenuous metaphor. This is the "Iliad" Homer would have written if he had known Krafft-Ebing.

The new poets

THE most provocative characters created by the poets of the advertising world recently were those two people with suntans who had just had a flying trip to Florida.

Man and woman, they kept cropping up in the papers and

on television flaunting their magnificent tans before sour and envious crowds of pasty-faced people who obviously wished them no good. Who are these two? What is their relationship? Is it aboveboard? And why did they fly to Florida?

The ad man who created them, the clever beguiler, tells nothing, but he leaves plenty to the imagination. As a servant to commerce, his primary purpose is to persuade everybody to buy an airplane seat from his client, Eastern Airlines, and go to Florida for a suntan. Like most good ad men, however, he is a poet at heart.

Working with a few meager symbols, he subtly suggests fully rounded characters that bloom and take life in the imagination. The ad men have been getting better and better at this. In fact, they may be creating the only really interesting characters in contemporary art, now that the novelists and playwrights have abandoned symbol and image for clinical exegesis.

Commander Whitehead and the man in the Hathaway shirt speak as eloquently of the American spirit in this century as Ahab and Miss Watson's Jim did in the last, and they are certainly more precise symbols of today's male than the supermen and psychopaths of the boudoir who fascinate the writers.

The charm of the ad men's better characters is that they arrest the imagination and grow. The man and woman with the suntans, for example, are obviously two distinctive human beings in an absorbing situation. At first glance, they appear to be man and wife. But then—look how she clings to him.

Marriage is obviously out. His wife would be waiting for him in the airport cocktail lounge. This girl may be in trouble. Close examination reveals that this is not just any man. This is a man who wears a tan camel's hair coat and is, therefore, probably a gangster or a theatrical agent.

The hostile expressions of the pasty-faced people help round out the characterization. These people clearly know him as an enemy of society. But what has brought him back from Florida to the land of the sallow? The triumphant smile suggests the answer. He is probably being promoted to a bigger job in Cosa Nostra up North.

Whatever the case, these are vital human beings with real problems. We want to know more about them; yet, like people in life, they have depths and ambiguities that can never be fully understood.

There is another tantalizing advertisement character who has been around awhile but becomes more fascinating with age. He wants a shot of whisky. Grant's scotch, to be precise. For years he has been sitting on a resort boardwalk with a typewriter on his lap asking someone to get him a Grant's.

Obviously well heeled (his typewriter is brand new) and dressed like a stage Englishman (ascot and blazer), he is clearly the wastrel heir of a Midwestern industrial family (probably Minneapolis) who is trying to muster courage to write home for more money. But what strange circumstance has brought the poor devil to this desolate sea resort where no one will being him a Grant's? Is he Odysseus in tennis shoes, or Prometheus chained?

Then there is the snarling middle-aged harridan—she needs a bromide—forever turning on her old mother and screaming, "I'd rather do it myself!" She is what Lady Macbeth might have become in a fully automatic kitchen, and the poet who created her knows his women as well as he knows his modern household management.

The character is flawed, of course, by the commercial necessity to effect an unconvincing quick cure with the bromide, but no one is deceived. We all know that this is a woman to be avoided.

The question is why we have to look to the ad men to create the representative characters of the age. Could it be because the ad men are studying man at grips with twentieth-century society, while the novelists and playwrights are busy examining the convolutions of navels?

Quickie

Two months before every Presidential campaign begins, Washington begins swarming with book publishers who trap you at lunch and seize you by the telephone with wild talk about big royalties and fifth printings. Before Election Day they mean to deluge the republic under campaign biographies of the statesmen who hope to guide our destinies.

As there are more publishers than Presidential candidates, the object is to see who can get his campaign biographies into the bookshops first. Speed is everything. At times like these, the publishers reduce literature to hamburger. Put some pulp between decorative cardboards and you can sate the customers while Boswell is still trying to wheedle an introduction to Johnson. So goes the theory, and practice has proved it financially sound.

Writing a "quickie" political biography, of course, is an art by itself and there is no point in sneering at it simply because it has nothing to do with literature. One of Washington's most prolific "quickie" biographers relaxed from his latest book recently long enough to discuss how he goes about it. Obviously, he can only be identified pseudonymously. Call him Smith.

"The important thing in a quickie," Smith said, "is striking a man-of-destiny note at the very outset." For this purpose, Smith keeps a complete opening "quickie" chapter all ready for the printer. It is entitled, "Born to Destiny."

The opening lines read like this: "The family knew that this was to be no ordinary baby. The elements themselves seemed to sense that they were attending an event of destiny and when little ——————— first blinked at the light of the world, his father felt a strange interior shudder and immediately sensed that this child was born for greatness . . ."

When the publishers need a "quickie" quickly, Smith has only to fill in the blanks with the name of the subject and send a completed first chapter to the printer by return mail. The second chapter, he says, is invariably the hardest. In this chapter, the "quickie" appraises what Smith calls "the whole man" as he is at the moment publishers find him marketable.

"This is slow work," Smith said. "You've got to know what the fellow looks like and a little something about what he's done and what other people think of him. This means a whole afternoon reading old newspaper clippings. Then you've got to get a look at him somehow and see how big he is and how much hair he has and what he does with his hands."

This chapter with all its research, often takes two or three days of work, although Smith confesses that he wrote his successful "quickie" on General MacArthur on the basis of interviews conducted over the span of two martinis at the National Press Club bar. "But MacArthur was such a vivid personality, that you could get the complete feel of him from a headline," he says.

Publishers usually like nine or ten other chapters to give the book weight. These are what Smith calls "the padding." He collects half the material by writing to the subject's enemies for their opinions and anecdotes. He next sends all this material to the subject's public relations man, who refutes it with other opinion and anecdote.

He then intertwines the two sets of opinion and anecdote without commentary. "This gives the impression that I am doing a cold, hard job of objective reporting," he says. "The reviewers always praise my stuff for its fairness and objectivity. 'Smith is a man who sees the bad as well as the good in ——————,' they always say."

In the concluding chapter, Smith likes to publish his own analysis of the man. In this, he says, he writes, "whereas on the one hand no one can deny, it is nevertheless obvious that quite the opposite is true too often to be ignored." And, "a man as complex as —————— cannot be entirely understood in terms of" and finally, "even his bitterest enemies must grant that he contains the seeds of greatness."

45

A check of Smith's works shows that he has used the identical chapter to conclude his biographies of Henry Wallace, General MacArthur, Ezra Taft Benson, Hubert H. Humphrey, and Mrs. Perle Mesta, which was admittedly a slow seller.

In 1964, Smith broke all records by writing biographies of seven Republican candidates, Lyndon Johnson, Moise Tshombe and four members of the Kennedy clan, all in a period of three months. Wherever the headlines may strike next, Smith will be ready with a biography. We are all looking forward to it, with plenty of catsup.

The Otto Awards

Another season of prize-giving is ending. We have had "Emmy," "Tony," "Oscar," the Pulitzers, the Nobels, the National Book Awards, the Heisman Trophy, the most valuable player, the rookie of the year, the Queen's honors list, the Lenin Prizes and, way back there, Miss America and Miss Universe, to name only a few.

The number of prizes available is constantly expanding, and the number of categories that each prize may honor is astounding. ("Best bongo effects for a regular weekly sponsored hospital drama," "Best choreography in a black-and-white foreign-language musical," etc.)

Surprisingly, however, there are still people who have never won a single prize for anything. Something should be done for these people. They are important to society. They do not do things, and the things they do not do very often make this a better world to live in.

To honor their achievements, let us establish a new prize, to be called "Otto," in memory of Professor Otto von Auserbei, who decided in 1937 not to send Adolf Hitler a memo explaining that atomic fission could be exploited to

46

make a bigger bomb for the *Luftwaffe*. ("I didn't want to annoy the Führer with detail," he later wrote.)

The following nominations for the 1965 Otto awards are not all-inclusive, but only designed to indicate the prize's scope:

For art: Hanson Cranksham, an insurance agent of Bergenfield, N. J. While drinking alone at home one evening—his wife had gone to a movie—Cranksham removed several wheels of New York cheddar cheese from the pantry, hung them on the living room wall and threw several dozen kitchen utensils into them. Fearing his wife's reaction, Cranksham removed the utensils and put the cheeses back in the pantry, thus sparing the world a new development in modern art.

For Washington correspondence: Giles Simpson of Simpson newspapers, who did not write a single line about Luci Baines Johnson's dancing habits.

For humanitarianism: Morton Decoverly of Ponderosa, Calif. Desperate for work, Decoverly, two hours after becoming an encyclopedia salesman, balked at making his first house call, threw his samples down a storm drain and went south to pick beans.

For peace: Nils Amstergaard, the Scandanavian explorer. In his travels somewhere east of the Congo, Amstergaard stumbled upon two undiscovered tribes at war. Befriending one of the chiefs, he advised the fellow to send a plea to the United Nations for a mixed inspection commission and peacekeeping forces. These, he explained, would shortly be followed by Russian and American technicians who would compete to democratize the local jungle. The plea was written and given to Amstergaard to take to New York. En route to the Congo River, Amstergaard lost his way and has not been heard of since.

For architecture: Johnny Doe, a dropout of Brooklyn, N. Y. While rifling a construction shack on Third Avenue one evening, Johnny thoughtlessly dropped his cigarette among some oily rags, and decided not to pull a fire alarm. The resulting fire destroyed the shack, as well as the only set

47

of blueprints for twelve new office buildings under construction in midtown Manhattan.

For science: Sherman Waldorf, a dry cleaner of Edgewood Arsenal, Md. When Barry Hahn, researcher in biological warfare, absent-mindedly left the formula for a new liver-atrophying gas in some pants sent for pressing, Waldorf found it. Mystified by the chemical symbols, but suspecting that he would have to answer to the F.B.I. if it proved to be a classified paper, Waldorf made no protest when his janitor picked it up and took it to the incinerator.

Everyone will have a candidate or two for an "Otto," for everyone can think of something undone that has helped keep the world in equilibrium. That is the beauty of "Otto." Almost everybody deserves one, and nobody need any longer go without a prize.

Grandfather knew plenty

Most of the commentary on the Smithsonian Institution's new Museum of History and Technology has emphasized the architectural failure of the building itself, but what should also be said is that the exhibits inside are an unqualified success.

The failure here has not been with father and grandfather and their forebears, whose worldly goods are on display, but with ourselves. Our own generation is unable to build a shelter worthy of housing what the old people have left us.

And the quality of what they have left is very high indeed. Item for item, they had us beat nine times out of ten when it came to taste and beauty. The 1918 Oldsmobile which is on display is a case in point. With its top raked at an angle just jaunty enough for a sporting man but not too immodest for a lady, it makes the 1965 cars look like overweight heifers.

Superiority is not confined to the automobiles. The gleaming green and silver steam locomotive, the Mack truck with its camel-nose hood and solid tires, the six-door electric trolleys and the lace delicacy of the Victorian San Francisco cable car—these came from a race of builders.

Even their gas pumps were beauties. The new museum has one. It is a tall and willowy red number with a breathtakingly tapered waist and, at head level, a clear glass cylinder where a man could watch his gasoline bubble about until it entered the hose.

What has become of this gracious and charming lady? Surely there is none of her soul left in that squat mercantile ogre mounted in cement at the gas station, with dollar signs for eyeballs and a squalid little tax computer where his heart should be.

Everybody will have more respect for his elders after seeing the new collection. The old European criticism that they were a crowd of drab materialists was partially wrong at least. Materialists they may have been, but as is made clear here, it was a materialism that produced much beauty and grace.

It was also a materialism which aspired to endure, and this fact inevitably raises a troubling question about our own generation. What is our generation going to leave for the Smithsonian? What have we that will last long enough to interest our grandchildren?

Our goods fall apart after they are three years old; our houses after twenty. Our great buildings are done in glass and are designed to be torn down. We are leaving hardly any personal written record of our passage here; letter writing is dying as our lives are talked out over the telephone. There is something sneaky about us. It is almost as if we were determined to come and go without leaving a footprint. It is fitting that this should be the generation for which total annihilation is at last feasible.

And yet there should be something we can leave so that our grandchildren and great-great-grandchildren can come back to us, in their maturity, and try to understand us prop-

49

erly, as we can now go to the Smithsonian and see our fore-bears with fresh perspective.

What artifacts will we be able to leave? A big jet, perhaps, which is beautiful as well as complex. An electronic com-puter, a complete unassembled stereo rig, an aerosol bomb, a tube of gentlemen's hair oil, a princess telephone, an album of credit cards and, if nothing else at all, one beer can—empty.

To be properly exhibited, of course, in that remote day at the Smithsonian, the mid-twentieth century collection should fall to pieces and need replacing after every three years. All, that is, except the beer can. This should lie forever, unrusting, on a beautiful green lawn.

Places, Times

Autumn in New Hampshire

PIKE, N. H.—A cold wind out of Canada rattled across Vermont and shook the mountains until the birches bent and the elms quaked. It had rained the day before, and the wind that followed left the forests and the sky looking freshly laundered, but something profound and slightly disturbing had also happened.

On the mountains, patches of brown had begun to appear. Here and there the green was shot through with streaks of flaming red where the first maples were beginning to turn and along the roads the first dead leaves were already adrift. The sunlight was pale gold suffused with an end-of-summer sadness.

There may be another gasp of summer left, and afterward the autumn will be lovely here, and then there will be skiing, but this first warning that summer is dying was, as always, unsettling.

At summer resorts like this, people have invested their dreams and their hopes as well as their money in the summertime, and the first hint of autumn makes them wonder uneasily if the investment has been sound. Those who have been disappointed wonder if there is still time for something wonderful to happen before the clock strikes, and the whine of the wind mocks them with the reminder that it must soon be now or never.

In this pause between seasons it is the girls who are poignant. They come to places like this for a week or two to meet the boys. It is all ritualistically respectable; their motives are ingenuously feminine. At dusk, gowned and perfumed to break an old man's heart, they sit on the wooden porches wondering among themselves whether "anything will happen" and trying to be philosophical about the possibility that it won't.

"The way I look at it," one lovely girl was telling another the other night, "if something wonderful happened, good, but if nothing happens I've still had a pleasant week of swimming, tennis and sunshine."

A happening here is a meeting with a boy who will cultivate the friendship back in New York, Boston or Philadelphia, and, ideally, consent some day to marriage. Old-timers report that heavy romance on the scene is a rarity and that the resorts serve chiefly as meeting grounds.

The problem is a fairly new one peculiar to our citified culture. A New York girl, for example, has extremely limited prospects of meeting the light of her life in the city, where her social range may be limited to an office and an apartment block, and where the proprieties forbid accepting casual approaches from strangers.

Here, however, in the permissive, supervised atmosphere of a summer picnic ground, the girls are not only encouraged to meet everybody but criticized as spoilsports if they don't. The number of marriages that result is commonly a trade secret among resort managers, but it is said to be impressive.

Unfortunately for the girls, this has been an awkward week here. By one of those ugly quirks of chance, boys are in exceedingly short supply, and they know it.

"The men here are all acting like kings," one girl complained. "Of course we are," one of the kings confided privately at the bar the other evening, "and we can afford to." The kings are behaving badly.

The girls are lovely, the more so because their plight is so touching. At sunset they come out of their rooms and cottages in their beautiful gowns and beautiful hair and beautiful eyelashes and head for the verandah where the dance music is playing and the kings stroll.

If all these girls were to walk down Madison Avenue at cocktail time looking as they look here they would be snapped up and married in an instant. But back home such displays are impossible, and here the summer is ticking away.

Many, of course, have already converted some of the kings back to boys, but many more must stand on the porch, letting their eyes trail silently behind passing lords, wondering if their investment of dreams may yet end with something wonderful happening, and hating the cold wind that shakes the elms.

Later there will be autumn, which is exciting in New York, and the disappointments will fade, and the girls will start investing new dreams in next summer.

Indian summer in Deerfield

OLD DEERFIELD, MASS.—Visiting towns like Old Deerfield is one of the great American pastimes. It is supposed to be good for the spirit. Poets feel that these places are full of old ghosts with something to tell us if only we can find them and commune.

The poets are doubtless right about Deerfield, for this was once a place of blood and early death, and of agonies beyond the comprehension of contemporary tourist Americans. But today the ghosts are coming through only faintly. Their signals are too weak and their message is garbled.

When Deerfield was founded, sometime after 1666, there was no United States in North America. There were England and Holland and France and there were the Indian nations. In today's world, these people would be held in low esteem. The white men behaved very badly, as the evil European colonialists are said to have been doing lately in Africa and Asia, and the Indians were still a long way from national self-government.

In a more sensible age, the African-Asian bloc would have forced the United Nations to adopt a resolution. This would have ordered the colonialists to get out and leave America for the Indians. A three-man commission of neutralists, composed of Sweden, Burma and Ghana, would have held the continent in trust until Massasoit or King Philip could have put the Indian economy on its feet.

Unhappily, there was no United Nations to see that things were done properly, and colonialism was allowed to take its ugly course. The result was a barbarism much like the recurrent state of affairs in the Congo.

Here at Deerfield, for example, the English settlers lived in constant fear of the natives, who were likely to swoop down and massacre or mutilate them or carry them off into the jungles to the north.

Even at that time, the French were playing a tricky hand. One night in 1704, after filling the Indians with firewater, a French and Indian raiding party looted and burned the town and killed or captured half its population.

It is very difficult today to find a ghost in Deerfield to say what to make of its barbarous past. This may be because these old ghosts now realize that they were colonialist exploiters and feel ashamed of themselves. They probably fear that if they stood around under the spreading elms boasting of their courage and of what they did here, the United Nations would send a team to exorcise them.

In any event, the ghosts stay off the main street most of the time, and as a result it is hard to grasp how it must have been when the golden hills rustled with menace and central Massachusetts was wilder than the Congo.

What we have instead is the conventional New England colonial town immortalized by Norman Rockwell. Gloriously proportioned frame houses under magnificent elms. Deep silences. Leaves ankle deep on the lawns. A posh prep school for boys. Tweedy girls. Indian corn nailed to the doors. An olde shoppe selling pewter. Silver birch and russet oak.

What we have, in short, is every American's dream of the small town in the suburbs. It is a dream of security and warmth, and not a place where anybody can come to grips with the brutality of early American life or appreciate the courage of the old colonialists.

Nowadays the ghosts rarely wander beyond the town

burial ground overlooking the Deerfield Academy football field, and even there they speak with forked tongues. There is the grave of Lieut. Mehuman Hinsdell, the first boy born here, noting enigmatically on his headstone that he was "twice captivated by Indian savages." But how did he twice escape?

And there is the smirking message from John Hunter, who died in 1787. "Look and behold as you pass by," Hunter urges. "As you are now, so once was I. As I am now, so you must be. Prepare for death and follow me."

A United Nations investigating team would probably conclude that such dreary philosophy typifies the colonialist mentality.

The faces of New York

NEW YORK—Where do New Yorkers get these faces that they wear in the streets of Manhattan? The variety is tonic, especially to anyone who has been drugged by the faces of Washington.

Washington is basically a one-face town. The typical Washington face has been scrutinized by the security police and certified non-eccentric by the Federal Government. There are roughly 250,000 such faces down there, and since each one must also have its wife and children pass Federal muster, the total number—man, woman and child—probably exceeds one million.

The other fifty per cent of the Washington population wears the basic Federal face because it is fashionable and for self-protection. After a while, you quit seeing these faces. After all, one safe face is pretty much like another.

Coming into Manhattan from such a place is to rediscover the human face. People walk the streets with the most star-

57

tling confessions written from chin to hairline. For anyone starved for the face of humanity, it is wonderful.

If there is one common characteristic of the New York face, it is disengagement from all other faces. It will not look at you. You can stand on a street corner and stare it right in the eyes, and it will refuse to see you.

A Washington face, when stared into, will check itself ostentatiously. You can watch it start to worry, to ask itself, "Is there ink on my nose?" or "Has the F.B.I. heard that my wife sneered at the Un-American Activities Committee last week?"

New York faces, on the other hand, remain perfectly composed no matter how closely examined. They refuse to have their privacy disturbed.

This is true only on the street, of course. In social or business contact, the New Yorker puts off his street face and gives himself freely. Indeed, he may be surprised and a little offended if told that he uses one face in public and another in private.

One of the most interesting places to watch faces is Times Square. Times Square faces tend, on the whole, to be slightly desperate. In the early evening there are the young, taut faces bent on picking up the illusory trail of pleasure. The happy imbecile faces grinning at the neon arcades. The faces of life's losers studying the lewd movie posters. The strained hungry faces of the boys who think that tonight, this night, something exciting may happen at last.

And there are the tourists' faces—harried, bland, intoxicated faces, in-from-Scarsdale faces, faces struggling to look like tough sophisticated New York faces, tired faces, betrayed faces.

These Times Square faces are mostly all, in their way, sad. The place is a microcosm of human aimlessness, and in the early morning hours, when the mob has thinned, there are the drifting, frustrated faces of the sleepless, resigned to tomorrow's hangover.

For an antidote there is the East Side, lair of the successful face. In Washington, the successful face may look a bit less worried than the crowd's, but in New York it is a face that boldly commands respect and stands out on the sidewalk.

Doormen, with their cunning, hooded faces so clever at appraising the price of your necktie, nod to these successful East Side faces and whistle up taxicabs for them. They are faces that transmit vital, tantalizing messages. "I am off to merge Consolidated," they say, without moving a jaw muscle. Or, "My prima ballerina has already been waiting 45 minutes."

For famous faces, Fifth Avenue is unbeatable. "Look," these Fifth Avenue faces say, "I am famous, and it's a great bore being looked at all the time, but see how unruffled I am by your stare." Famous faces are always either dashing into beauty salons, obviously late, or smiling at the best joke in the world which they have just heard.

There are more—the Village faces (Ohio faces wearing beards), Mets-fan faces (lippy, sad), Yankee-fan faces (smug), Mafia faces, theater faces, faces running on benzedrine and faces unsafe to walk with on a lonely street.

It would be good for the country to ship a large assortment of them to Washington, but it probably isn't in the cards.

Extreme Manhattan

NEW YORK—One of the agents whom Washington sends periodically to keep an eye on New York City granted the following interview at his hotel:

Q. Are you free to say, sir, what your mission is in New York?

A. This is what we call a passive surveillance. Inside American territory we have no operational authority like the boys have in, say, Saigon. I couldn't undertake to shore up the Wagner regime, for example, or undermine Adam Clayton Powell, or spread salt on the ice at the Rockefeller Center skating rink. That's operations. My job is just to keep my eyes open and report.

Q. What is Washington's attitude toward New York these days?

A. Frankly, it's not very happy about New York. I'm not revealing any classified material when I tell you that New York is regarded by Washington as one of the two greatest nuisances in the country.

Q. The other being. . . . ?

A. The Deep South. If Washington could normalize New York and the Deep South, this country would be a happier place, but it's impossible to finalize national tranquillity—domestic-wise, that is—while you've got all these agitators in New York and the Deep South constantly demanding their rights.

Q. Excessive insistence upon rights, I take it, disturbs Washington?

A. Nothing irritates Washington more than a lot of nuisances insisting on rights. They create bad feeling in the Senate clubrooms, spoil Presidential outings and make it harder for everybody to get re-elected. These are the people who turn out to be extremists on both sides.

Q. Washington is fearful of extremism on both sides?

A. It's the extremists on both sides who are making it impossible for reasonable men, men of goodwill, to reach sensible solutions in the great American tradition. Washington feels that the extremists on both sides may be as dangerous today as the Communists were last year.

Q. Have you seen an extremist on both sides here in New York?

A. It's hard to be certain. They don't carry cards, you see, but this is the kind of place that breeds them.

Q. I suppose you refer to the high concentration of political liberals in New York?

A. Well, the place has always been full of liberals, as they call themselves. In Washington, we call them crackpots, knee-jerks, do-gooders. Down there we know how to handle them.

60

Q. You let the do-badders give the do-gooders a lesson about the great American tradition, I assume?

A. Politics is not my responsibility. I see and report. That's all.

Q. Can you reveal what tendencies toward extremism on both sides you have noted here this week?

A. The town is a hotbed of extremist tendency. This morning as I went down to breakfast, I happened to glance into the bar. There were three men—at 8 o'clock in the morning, mind you—drinking martinis.

Q. But this hotel is on Madison Avenue. . . .

A. That is not all. At 10:20 P.M. last night while walking at 85th Street and Second Avenue, I saw a young couple walking across an intersection with a large sofa. Yesterday during the afternoon rush hour at 42nd Street and Lexington Avenue, a woman was screaming at the crowds that kidnappers were stealing babies from incubators, and not a soul looked at her.

Q. What will Washington make of all these phenomena?

A. We can safely say that Washington will not be reassured. Imagine how you would react if you were responsible for the national security and received reports that there was a place in this country where martinis were drunk unashamedly in public at 8 A.M., where couples went walking with sofas after dinner, and where no one was interested in screams about kidnapping?

Q. I suppose I would say, "Everything seems normal in New York." Wouldn't you?

A. Ah, so? I am afraid that Washington will be interested in having your name. No resistance, please. I am authorized to act forcibly. . . .

August on the Mississippi

MEMPHIS, TENN.—Somebody is always trying to pacify the Mississippi River with sweet talk. This is ludicrous. The Mississippi is not only the meanest, but also the trickiest brute on the continent, and the sensible way to deal with him is to call off the poets and bring in somebody like Dr. Edward Teller.

Popular imagination has been so steeped in romance about "Ol' Man River" and "The Father of the Waters" that the true nature of Mississippi-ism is understood by scarcely a handful of Americans.

The fact is that the Mississippi has constantly defied the authority of the United States Government, has resisted the march of electronic-concrete civilization, has destroyed towns and refused to cooperate with automotive authority and has successfully stayed at war with the United States Army longer than any other power in history.

The river is also a sneak-thief. While politicians vow to protect every inch of free soil against Communist seizure, the Mississippi is constantly picking up huge chunks of Pittsburgh, Minnesota and the Dakotas and shipping them down to Arkansas or throwing them out in the sea.

Right now, the river is in one of its docile moods, murmuring about coexistence and insisting that it doesn't really mean to bury us at all. Its level the other evening when Capt. Tom Meanley took the Memphis Queen downstream with a load of sightseers was at the lowest point of the year and still falling.

Captain Meanley, who has to live with the river, addressed it with respect. "Ol' Man River is mighty low today," he said, loud enough for the river to hear the diplomatic tone of his voice. The river smirked slyly, and slapped a little of stolen Minnesota against the Memphis Queen's bow.

By way of propitiating the thing, the captain played a

vocal rendition of "Ol' Man River" over the boat's amplifier and maintained a courteous silence until the last note had faded into the Arkansas willows.

Memphis, standing back on the high Chickasaw bluffs, slid away. The Mississippi writhed in a huge serpentine coil and, with Memphis gone, exposed a vista of unutterable loneliness. The old river towns that once dotted the river every five or six miles are almost all gone now.

Below Memphis, the river snakes through wilderness on both banks for 72 miles until it comes to Helena, Ark. There is scarcely a ghost town any longer to preserve the memory of steamboat days, though people who venture into the wild may occasionally find a clump of chimney tops jutting out of the silt.

The defeat of civilization along the banks is one of the prices the country has had to pay in its constant war with the river. As the levees rose upstream to contain the bed, the water volume increased downstream until the riverfront towns had to be sacrificed. Down there, the levees were built behind the towns. So were the railroads, as steamboat traffic waned, and the towns literally went under.

The highways, too, are kept at respectful distance. As a result, the Misissippi boasts the only victory of this century over the highway builders. It tolerates no scenic highway for lazy eyes to violate its privacy.

Along the so-called "Great River Road" from Cairo, Ill., to Memphis there is only one point where the motorist can glimpse the river. And that glimpse lasts less than a minute.

There are a million acres of wilderness between Cairo and Memphis alone. Here the whim of the Mississippi is absolute. Though there is only one passenger steamer left on the whole river, the snub-nosed diesels haul more freight than in Mark Twain's day.

The men who work on the diesels insist that it isn't really lonely, but this is probably nothing more than the normal discretion of people who have to do business with a hostile power. In midstream, from the deck of the tiny Memphis

Queen, it is full of evil smiles about towns it has buried and the outrages it will commit in the spring.

One of these days, it knows, it is going to have the last laugh. It may take awhile, but time, it figures, is on its side.

Two days to Denver

DENVER—Here is a fascinating new idea in travel. It is called the train. It is marvelous. It hugs the earth and bears you along at one-tenth the speed of sound, with frequent stops to allow close scrutiny of the American landscape.

It is especially recommended for the ruling classes, who suffer from the delusion that being shot across the continent in a metal cylinder is the ultimate in fancy living.

A substantial train trip—as from Washington to Denver—takes two nights. Trains provide ingenious private rooms complete with plumbing and beds. Seasoned air travelers will be delighted to find that, once seated or reclining in these rooms, privacy is absolute.

Young women with glass smiles do not barge in to ask if a seatbelt is fastened, or to offer chewing gum, or to push coffee, tea and milk.

The fast trains west out of Washington depart at tea time. There is no luggage weigh-in at the terminal and no psychic compulsion to buy $65,000 worth of life insurance before boarding, though the first few hours may put heavy strains on the person unaccustomed to train travel.

After half an hour—a period in which a traveler from Washington would normally expect to be approaching Pittsburgh—he may start wandering the train nervously, asking how far it has gone. It will be just outside Silver Spring, Md., perhaps 20 miles beyond Washington.

As the evening wears on and the diesels start their labored

curve over the Appalachians, he will discover the diner and the lounge and begin to notice features of America that are invisible from 30,000 feet. That the Eastern countryside is carpeted with black-eyed susans. That country children still stand by railroad tracks to wave at people bound for Chicago.

And then, with nightfall, the train is a cocoon of soft light rushing through the starred tunnel of night, its whistle baying at mountain towns. Over the rough Appalachian roadbed, the thing creaks and groans like a ship at sea, and in the black hours, with a screech and jolt of brakes, it wakes the sleeper to witness the fires of Pittsburgh.

With morning, it is racing across the Indiana flatlands and by breakfast it is gliding into the steel labyrinth of Chicago, already shimmering under a hot brass sky. It is still necessary to change trains to cross the Mississippi. The explanation is a mystery to all but railroad men. Hogs can cross the continent without changing trains, as someone used to say, but people can't.

The result is a day of toil. Baggage must be unloaded, shipped to another station, stored. Hours must be killed in Chicago. Nobody can say for certain how many hours, for the trains have their own time, and only mathematicians understand it.

In Chicago it is 98 degrees in the shade. The streets are melting. The traveler begins to curse the train. And, also to feel heroic about making such a hardship journey West.

Back to the station through layers of heat for the night train to Denver. Get the baggage out of storage. Fight for a baggage cart. Then, agony. The train leaves at 5 P.M., central standard time, and not 5 P.M., central daylight time. Another steaming hour to kill with the baggage. Do not ask why the trains refuse to operate on local time. It is a mystery, like why they force people to change in Chicago. The trains have their dignity. They do not put themselves out for people.

And then, at last, it is moving again through the dusk. Across the Mississippi and into Iowa and hurtling down

65

across Nebraska, restoring serenity. By morning it is in a new world of vast crystal sky and sage-brush, pounding toward the Rocky Mountains.

Fifty miles across the prairie, the peaks are still creased with snow. At Denver the air is hot, dry and sparkling, and the westering man who could have made the whole trip in five hours by jet arrives with a sense of having made an expedition.

He has not merely been on an elevator ride. He has traveled, and he feels it. Two whole days from Washington to Denver! The pioneers couldn't have arrived with a greater sense of pride.

July on the Oregon Trail

PENDLETON, ORE.—Back down the road a piece, along the Snake River, there was a grizzled mirage standing in the sage-brush. There was nothing to do but photograph him, but he was obviously uneasy and it was necessary to jolly him along with small talk.

"Hello, there, old-timer. You're a mirage, aren't you?"

"Yup," he said.

"Lost?"

"I'm looking for the Oregon Trail," he said. "You haven't seen the wagons along this way by any chance?"

"Well, you see, old-timer, we don't travel by wagon train any more. Nowadays we have cars." He looked nonplused. "See that box sitting over there on wheels? That's a car. It goes six hundred miles a day. When you people wanted to get to Oregon it took you five months from Missouri. We make it now in three days."

He whistled in disbelief. "What's it like?" he asked. "Traveling in one of those cars, I mean."

"Why, man, it's the only way to see the country. I get in

Eventually they arrive at places like this. It is a gigantic shopping center with little rental houses for the customers. In fact, it is just like home, except that the houses are painted lavender and orange to match the customer's clothing.

Then everyone concentrates on having a wonderful time. There are many obstacles, psychological as well as material, to be hurdled before a wonderful time can really be enjoyed.

First off, there is the problem of walking around in public in those ridiculous pink and yellow clothes. Everybody else is wearing them, but then everybody else looks funny, too, in an ugly way. The problem about these clothes is not only that the colors are hideous, but also that they feel, on the wearer, like underwear.

Most people find it hard to have a wonderful time when they feel that they are walking along crowded streets in their underwear, and it takes an act of courage to get out of the house the first few times.

It makes it no easier on the vacationer to go out in these clothes and find that everyone is staring at him. The reason is that the newcomers are usually very white in comparison to the seasoned vacationers, all of whom are darkened to the shade of well-traveled alligator suitcases.

The vacationer feels terrible about being pale. Pale skin marks him as a tourist, and the worst thing about being a tourist is having other tourists recognize you as a tourist. And so, for three or four days, he broils himself mercilessly in the sun, suffering the contemptuous smiles of the tan people, hoping that he will eventually become inconspicuous enough to have a wonderful time.

The children, being children, have no sympathy for their elders' problems. The parent who wants to broil himself in the secrecy of the backyard before making a public appearance is beset by his children, who want to get on with the wonderful time immediately.

If one child wants to go to the swimming pool, the other insists on the beach. There is nothing to do but go to both places, feeling hot, pale and underwear-conscious. The pool

69

swarms with millions of bodies, for the whole exploded American population is fighting to get to the ocean so that it can swim in a pool.

It is impossible to get into the pool without a shoehorn, and once in, it is impossible to do more than stand packed among bodies, feeling wet, pale and overcrowded. At the poolside, bronzed godlets play Liverpool rock 'n' roll on their transistor radios, adding to the din.

The ocean's emptiness is a blessing. If only it weren't a half mile walk across the furnace of the shopping center's asphalt tarmac. And then, of course, the body must be coated in grease and sheltered under canvas after thirty minutes of exposure. If the skin burns, it will later peel off in sheets and everyone will be scandalized. It isn't easy having a wonderful time.

Later there will be a drive on the beach with the car. It is the thing to do here. The sand and salt corrode the finish and get into those thousands of tiny moving parts, but it is all part of having a wonderful time; the auto repair shops love it.

How good it will be when the wonderful time has been had, and the car is repaired, and the tan has bleached to white, and the pink and yellow clothes are all burned.

Chilly on the Gold Coast

DAYTONA BEACH, FLA.—It is chilly in these motels. Someone has cut off the past, and there is nothing here but the air-conditioned present. People pay good money to sit in it. You see them now and then peeping through the slats of the venetian blinds. Something about it is wrong.

It is the tourist season on this coast and the place is full of Georgians and Carolinians. They come and sit in the motels. The motels are disturbing. Motels should be way stations on the road to Someplace, a compromise with the discomfort of transit, but here they are the end of the line, the reason for travel. The means have become the end.

Outside it is hot, whenever it is not raining. It is necessary to go out periodically. The air-conditioning affects the nerves after a while; one longs to escape its damp vapors and constant hum. Moreover, with the car in the breezeway, the motel psychology compels nervous movement.

There are many places to drive to. Some people drive into the swamps and look at alligators. The alligators have a stabilizing influence. Most of them have been here longer than most of the citizenry, and they help offset the feeling that the whole state was built last week.

The motorist can also drive to the beach. The surf is refreshing, the beach boys are picturesque, and it is exciting watching the airplanes skim the waves dragging commercial messages for cocktail lounges, or seeing the surf toss the garbage back onto the beach.

At night people bet on the dog races and jai alai and sit in these motels feeling chilly, watching television and peeping through the slats of the venetian blinds.

If all this is the American dream of the good life, and Florida's success suggests that it is, the question is whether the good life is good enough. Florida tourism is built on the theory that what we want to do with our leisure time is to invest it entirely in relishing the present moment. Its goal is total fun in total comfort.

There is a lot to be said for fun and comfort, but total fun and total comfort wind up by being total bores, and in the process pleasure is lost. Writing in the Bulletin of the New York Academy of Medicine, Alexander Reid Martin recently stated that new labor-saving machines have brought us to a new "adventure in free time" for which we are poorly equipped.

"Leisure," he adds, "is not the inevitable result of spare time, a holiday, weekend or vacation. It is, in the first place, a particular state or condition of mind and being—more specifically, an actively receptive condition of the whole personality."

The trouble here is that "the whole personality" tends to get overwhelmed by the fun and comfort. A romp in the surf may be good for it, but what happens to it when it steps out of the water and has to start worrying about the automobile traffic moving along the beach?

The time-honored method for whipping the whole personality into an actively receptive condition is to bring it out of the surf, rest it on an isolated dune, and let it wander idly through its own history.

Forcing it to dodge automobiles on the beach won't do. Putting it into its own car and driving it back to its motel disrupts the whole process, especially when that chilled air strikes the wet body.

Driving it into the swamps to commune with alligators may be helpful, but not if it makes the trip merely because the car and the motel are insistent. Betting on jai alai and dog races might help too (though it seems doubtful) but they are useless if undertaken only because they are an advertised part of the total fun.

But this seems unappreciative of Florida, and it should not be. When all is said and done, it is fun here sitting in the air-conditioning, itching to get out among the alligators.

Let us peep through the slats of the venetian blinds and see how hot it looks out there.

Labor Day on the turnpike

SOMEWHERE-ON-THE-TURNPIKES—How good it is to have a holiday. The car loves it, especially on these magnificent new turnpikes.

It has been racing happily over the concrete for hours now, nipping at Volkswagens and taunting stolid old tractor-

72

trailers. Now and then, it pauses for a gasoline refresher or an oil gargle, but it refuses to remain kenneled long when there is holidaying to be had, and it races eagerly back to the fast lane as soon as its thirst is slaked.

Actually, it was probably a mistake to let the car go out today. Its radio keeps shouting that death is imminent for car lovers all over the country, and it is difficult to enjoy a fast five hundred with the car when the radio is in its doomsday mood.

Still, a holiday is a holiday, and what is it for if not to treat the car to a romp? It is good for the master, too. Oh, not that it's pleasant—far from it—but it's broadening. Thirty years ago, a man and his car out on holiday felt that they had been somewhere if they went from Nutley to Singac, N. J.

Nowadays the two of them can race from Miami to Rocky Mount, N. C., or from Saratoga, N. Y., to Havre de Grace, Md., in the time it used to take to get to Singac and back to Nutley. We owe all this to the splendid new turnpike system, and nobody can drive five hundred miles for a swim without reflecting upon how far America has come in thirty years and sensing that the Russians are still in the Nutley-to-Singac era.

Actually, if it were not for the pride and wonder of it, these frolics with the car would be almost unbearable for the master. At this very moment, for example, the car seems to know precisely where it is and to enjoy being here.

But where is it? The car cannot say. The speedometer shows that it is moving at seventy miles an hour. The clock shows that it is five-thirty in the afternoon. Two young men without shirts are drinking beer from cans and passing in a convertible in the fast lane.

They are gaping as though they had never seen anyone work a typewriter on a steering wheel before, yet they see nothing remarkable in using a convertible as a beer parlor. Perhaps this is Florida. It is hard to remember.

This is the problem about the turnpikes. For the first two or three hours, everything is very clear. The master knows that he has breakfasted in Havre de Grace and headed north,

73

or shaved in Chicago and headed east. After four or five hours of staring at asphalt, however, he begins to doze, then to lose track of time, then to hallucinate.

It would be sensible to pull off the road and do deep knee bends, but the car is enjoying itself so much that it seems a pity to spoil its fun. It is easier to throw the head back and scream.

The scream can be drowned by turning up the radio volume. The cars have been remarkably canny about their radios. The only thing these radios can play is the sound of people screaming, which makes it possible for the master to express himself freely without attracting stares from the crowd in the fast lane.

They say that out here on the turnpikes there are thousands of maddened motorists who have driven continuously for months, screaming from ocean to ocean, from prairie to bayou, and that sometimes in the night you can hear their cars scream back.

At 8 o'clock this morning—nearly ten hours ago—this very car was at Concord, N. H.—no, at Boulder, Colo. Yes, it must have been Boulder. There were fried potatoes on the eggs. And it was the Labor Day weekend, and it seemed like the American thing to take the car out and turn on the screams and perhaps drive over to Havre de Grace for a swim and feel superior because the Russians cannot drive from Moscow to Pinsk without storing gasoline in the trunk. . . .

In any case, there was that disturbing sign in midafternoon which said "Boston; 32 miles," and then there was that long period of dozing with the wonderful dream about having to drive only from Nutley to Singac to get a swim.

Ah well, why be peevish? It is wonderful for the cars, and they enjoy it so much.

July in the other America

WASHINGTON, July, 1964—What is there to say of the America that is not in the headlines this barbarous July? Very little that is new, and nothing that will stir the passions like the overstatement of the political campaign, the rioting in Manhattan and Florida, the hatred in Mississippi.

And yet it is still there, this other country which makes no headlines. You can go out across the continent all the way to the Pacific, and look at it, and stand in it, and touch it, and be moved, awed and amused by it. The trouble is that there is nothing to report from it.

Consider the Mendocino coast of northern California. It is a place of important things not worth reporting. Several eons ago nature went wild and heaved the beaches high above the level of the sea and gradually turned them into meadows. The serenity is absolute.

In the morning fog deer prance in the cemeteries. Nights are chill and misty. Woolens are required. The Pacific placidly eats at the rock. News of the latest rioting in the other America seeps in only slowly, brought by San Franciscans come to have their nerves wound down. It feels a long way to Mississippi, but what else is there to say of it?

Wyoming presents the same problem. The news from Wyoming is that there is nobody there. Or hardly anybody. The train travels a hundred miles between human faces across a deserted moonscape of boulder and scrub, snaking along cracked dry river beds and vistas of ruined cliffs crumbling to dust.

Occasionally the train stops. Big men with sunburned faces and big hats climb aboard. Their immediate problem is the beef glut. The West is suffering from a beef explosion that has almost doubled the cattle population since 1950, but the great dull problem that will plague America long after this summer's riots are forgotten is water.

75

If there were water the West would inherit the earth, but everyone knows that, and what else is there to say? It is one of those tediously enduring problems that plague this other country and seldom engage the attention 'of a world ready to accept the snarl of the mob as the true face of America.

And Iowa. Something important should be said about Iowa. But what is there to say? Iowa is an emotional experience. The beautifully ordered farms, the summer billow of green corn, the floating haze of wildflowers—these things evoke a hopeless sense of regret for the history that has moved America off the land and into the cities.

The towns of Iowa, with their tree-lined squares and upright homes and vegetable gardens in the back yards—these towns are towns out of the memories of childhood.

The mood is not all sentimentality, of course. In Chicago it may be the beery conviviality of a touring group of Milwaukee Braves boosters pausing to rag a Polish bartender about the inferiority of the Chicago Cubs. These other Americans still care more about baseball than about ideology and spend more energy hating the other pitcher than hating the man across town.

They are also predominantly proud of their places that never make the headlines. "How do you like our redwoods?" the waitress at a hamburger stand in the Sequoia country will ask with a pride that brooks nothing but the most outrageous cries of admiration for *Sequoia sempervirens.*

All are part of the American fiber and they temper the natural strain of violence which has always been part of the American character. It is helpful, during a July like this one, to remind ourselves that there is, as always, another America, and that it is the one in which most Americans live most of the time.

Fortunately, there is very little to say of it that is new, and nothing that will stir the passions.

IV

Some American Pastimes

Staying hip

The new catalogue of next year's things is just out, and it's enough to make a person give up and resign himself to being passé. Staying hip next year will be harder than ever before. Most of this year's things are out. Extremism, the frug, the watusi, the swim, hair curlers, pop art, black humor, the Beatles, drinks on the rocks—these are just a few of this year's things that have been dropped altogether or modified so radically that next year's versions will be barely recognizable.

Take dancing. The new dances will be the swarm and the smoke. The smoke will be a relief to older people who want to stay with it. Danced barefoot, its basic motion is achieved by pretending to walk on a bed of live coals while holding lighted cigarettes in both hands, inhaling them alternately and blowing the smoke over your partner's ear.

As for the swarm—well, people who thought the frug was demanding haven't seen anything yet. The important new feature is that partners dancing the swarm never rejoin each other again after the dance is over. Thus, it is a dance which expresses the fundamental senselessness of dancing in an age of lonely quiverers.

The Beatles have turned out to be charming, but they're out for next year. Unfortunately for them, parents have come to like them. The big singing thing next year will be the Mechanarchists, a brilliant new trio from the West Coast who play the motorcycle cylinder, twin exhaust pipes and the punctured muffler.

The ladies will be glad to learn that they will no longer have to go to the supermarket wearing those big hair curlers the color of wet bubble gum. The new supermarket thing defies description. Suffice it to say that there is a geat deal of plastic hosing and aluminum involved.

79

The new thing in art will not be "found art"—the school begun recently by a Baltimorean who hung a weathered garage window cover he had found. It will be charred art; that is, objects recovered by fire departments which have been burnt into perceptive expressions of modern man's plight.

Few people will complain about the demise of drinks on the rocks. Next year, the thing will be rocks on the side. The rocks will no longer be ice cubes, but genuine rocks. To be absolutely with it, the hostess will want to have a set of imported rocks bearing London labels. It will be expensive, but it will be worth it to have an honest drink again and still be in fashion.

Black humor will not be exactly out next year. What they're going to do is take black humor all the way by eliminating the humor. What will be left will be black, black, black. People will sit in black theaters waiting for curtains that never go up, buy books inked with solid black pages. Everybody will think black. It will be a side-splitting expression of opposition to life.

Many people will probably decide that they simply cannot go on staying with it next year. Every year a certain percentage of hipsters drops by the wayside, refusing to give up last year's things, insisting that this year's things go too far.

These people keep a body of traditionalism alive in the country. They are the people who help preserve such institutions as Guy Lombardo, Elvis Presley, hair knots for women with lovely necks, Pablo Picasso and Jackson Pollock, the fox trot and the twist, the martini olive and Everett McKinley Dirksen.

We would be poorer without these institutions, no doubt, but it is the people who manfully buck up to coping with next year's things who keep us going. As a class they are not fools. They simply operate on the assumption that even though things will get worse, somebody has to make the most of it.

Hi fi

The old record player quit working. The young man at Sound Sound Systems was insulted. "A record player?" he asked. "You want a record player?" Two *aficionados* of pure sound modulated their woofers and offered supercilious smiles.

"People who want record players," said the young Sound Sound man, "go to drugstores." Apologies were offered. "I have a degree in hysteresis-synchronous motor utilization from the Massachusetts Institute of Technology," the young man said.

"I'm sorry." "Are you interested in a sound system?" "Will it play Errol Garner records?"

"Listen," said the hysteresis-synchronous motor utilization scholar. He led the way to an enormous control panel, buckled himself into the pilot's seat, made radio contact with the tower and began flicking switches while two men ran up and stood by on either side with fire extinguishers.

In a moment the shop was tingling with sound. "Is that sound?" he asked with an expression demanding rhapsodic agreement, "or is that sound?"

"Magnificent! But what is it?" "Sound!" he exulted. "Pure unblemished transistorized amplified sound! This particular system uses a transistorized control center with gold-plated circuitry and has plug-in epoxy panels for fully modulated efficiency. With a solid-state amplifier specifically mated to the loudspeaker-enclosure combination and a vibration-absorbing suspension system, it should play Errol Garner to a king's taste."

It seemed pretentious. "How about something in a three-way infinite baffle unit?" he asked. "Here we have a system employing two 16-ohm woofers, one midranger and a minor galaxy of broad-dispersion treble speakers. Its price is $595, plus installation charges, and for $295 more you receive an

81

18-month correspondence course in electronics which should eventually qualify you to operate it."

"Whatever happened to the old Victrola?"

"Ah," said the young man, his face radiant with understanding. "You are looking for a stereo amplifier. You should have said so."

He bounded off among an assortment of electronic equipment. "This one delivers 40 watts per channel with maximum harmonic distortion of 0.6 per cent from 13 to 30,000 cps. We recommend mating it with a two-way bass reflex speaker system containing two new high-compliance bass speakers, sectoral horn driven by high-frequency driver and an 800-cycle dividing network."

It looked terribly expensive, but in this strange language it was difficult to argue. Still, it seemed bad policy to act the complete ignoramus. One had to show that he knew a thing or two. "All very well, young man, but what about the preamp?"

He immediately went defensive. "All right," he conceded, "this system can be overloaded at the input by some current high-grade pickups, but to avoid distortion we will connect an attenuator, reducing pickup sensitivity to no more than 2 mv/cm/sec."

"I don't want to have any attenuators put on Errol Garner."

"With electrically self-defeating tone controls and a transformerless output of 35 watts per channel, plus a loudness compensation circuit phased in with rumble and scratch filters, you'll hardly notice any attenuation at all of Errol Garner. Of course, we make no guarantee unless the components are sited by our sound architects."

It had begun to look as if honorable escape was impossible when suddenly there was a rumbling explosion and fire broke out in number four tweeter, plunging the shop into a perilous neck-snapping spin.

While the young man fought with the infinite baffle control panel, it was child's play to duck out the back door and run home. After school the children were sent to the drugstore for a record player.

Decorating

The fact that Andrew S. (he asks to remain anonymous) has canceled plans to vacation on Antigua next month is of no importance to the public, but his reasons for doing so cast interesting light on the trials of middle-class living. In a letter he writes as follows:

Let me say at the outset that I am one of life's most consistent losers. Although I have been moderately successful at my work and earn a comfortable living, I am basically the sort of person to whom nothing good has ever happened.

Without belaboring the point I will simply note that the first car I ever owned was the last Hudson ever made, and that my second was an Edsel. It should be obvious that I am a man of considerable pessimism and negligible expectations.

Accordingly, when my wife and I decided last autumn to splurge on a winter in Antigua, I hadn't the least hope that the thing would come off, but I was mildly curious to see what disaster would intervene. Well, sir, it started with finger smudges on the stairway wall. But let me backtrack a bit.

Two years ago we were living in a small box in the suburbs. The children had begun to grow leggy and I had developed this terrible sensation of living a totally boxed life. Inside our box we were all cramped into small interior boxes filled with even smaller boxes.

One could stare at the box that talked, or go into the kitchen and ponder the box that cooked, or escape on the box with wheels. My analyst diagnosed a dangerous obsession and advised a move. And so we sold the place and bought an enormous old box of the kind they don't build any more.

The sense of enboxment subsided at once, and I even began to develop a fondness for the old place. Well, as I was saying, we had booked for Antigua when my wife remarked on the finger smudges on the stairway wall paint.

"We must have this wall papered with something washable," she said, and called a wallpaper man. When he arrived he shook his head mournfully and warned that it would be a bad mistake to paper until certain cracks in the plaster had been repaired.

My wife called a plasterer, who agreed to examine the cracks within a fortnight. "Hm," he said, "you've really got cracks. Bad cracks." My wife, who was naturally alarmed, asked him to examine the really prepossessing cracks which we had always taken for granted in the north bedrooms and shower stall.

"Yes, sir," he said, "these are really some cracks." "What do you think caused them?" asked my wife. "Could be," he mused, "you got termites under the north end of the house and they've eaten away all the underpinnings."

He thought it would be a mistake to undertake major crack repairs until the foundation had been thoroughly examined. Seven weeks later a carpenter agreed to give us an appointment. At the north end of the cellar he tore away some beaverboard ceiling and exposed perhaps twelve feet of suspended sawdust.

"You had termites, all right," he allowed. "Look at this beam." He handed me a palm full of sawdust. "Will the dining room fall through?" asked my wife. "Not so long as you stay out of there," he said.

He thought that the damage was reparable, although it would require electricians to relocate the overhead wiring during the operation. The cost? "It'll be a right good bit," he said. "About the cost of a month in Antigua?" I asked. "Just about," he thought.

"Of course," he went on, "it would be foolish to undertake elaborate repairs until the exterminator has got rid of any termites that might still be around." The exterminator's estimate arrived last month. It was for $261.35, but the exterminator thought it would be foolish to have the job done before we had the rainspout people and a landscape gardener do something about the drainage problem at the foundations.

84

The rainspout man was here yesterday. He says the roof is in bad shape and ought to be replaced. My wife telephoned a roofer this morning. Right after she canceled our bookings in Antigua. Next year, she says, we will go to Spain. Unfortunately, I am not getting any younger.

Losing

There has been a quiet undercurrent of amusement for the last few years in Washington over the bush-league exhibitionism of the New York Mets baseball fans.

The Washington baseball fan, who is perhaps the most civilized citizen of the modern sports world, has had thirty years of experience in the art of living with a bunch of bums, and it is obvious to him that New Yorkers are going about it all wrong.

You hear it said here that New York fans take no real pride in occupying the National League cellar. That they go to the park like gullible rubes, expecting an athletic contest. That they really aspire to the shabby distinction of finishing eighth or seventh, and have juvenile fantasies of winning a pennant some day.

Washington fans are particularly amused by the New York boasting about the Mets' record number of losses for a single season. This, they say, is a trifling distinction compared with the Senators' 30-year record of total incompetence.

A few years ago, when signs of professionalism began to occur on the Senators, the whole team was promptly transferred to Minnesota. Awesome sums were then spent to assemble what looked like the worst team money could buy—until the Mets arrived.

This didn't distress the Washington fan, who is at heart a philosopher with a distaste for the crudities of competition. He goes to the park for esthetic reasons. "Come out and see beautiful D. C. Stadium," is the constant plea of the game announcers. A plea to "come out and see the Senators" would set the whole town laughing.

The Washington fan is like a ballet-goer. He knows the tragic plot by heart, but attends to savor the artistry of the performance. Will Mr. Maris's three-run homer be cleanly stroked into deep right-center, or be one of those cheap Chinese homers down the foul line?

When the Senators blow the five-run lead in the ninth, will it be done in the classic comic spirit with ingeniously contrived errors, or will the pitcher simply yield hit after hit until the Yankees exhaust themselves running bases?

What the Washington fan talks about fondly are old losing streaks. It is nothing to remember details of a ten-game losing streak. These recur throughout every summer. The great streaks last sixteen or seventeen games. Washingtonians around the world follow them avidly, boast about them to strangers and tell one another that there has never been such a losing streak before.

The Washington fan has discovered the deeper wisdom of baseball. He knows from long experience that it is, after all, a bore, like the Western movie, which always follows the same script.

The Yankees will win and the Senators will lose just as surely as the white hat will gun down the black hat in the last reel. The teams destined to float between second and ninth place have never conceded the immutability of their fates.

They are the comic relief, the good fellows who can't quite bust broncs with the best, the corrupt sheriffs in cahoots with saloonkeepers. They are forever optimists, praying for a fluke, insistent on hope. The plot is a terrible bore, but the wonderful trick is that it repeats itself by mysterious natural law each year.

The universe is expanding; the earth is coming unstitched; geniuses boggle at the complexity of modern life. And yet everything is comfortingly unchanged in the tiny, stable, non-expanding universe of baseball.

Consider the last thirty years. Over that period Russians

have been bad, then good, then bad again. Germans were bad, then good. Chinese were good, then bad. Japanese were bad, then good. One thing, however, is just the same this year as it was in the mid-thirties: the Senators are still faithfully losing.

To the Washington fan, the Senators are a comforting fixed point in a small but safe world. Urbane men cherish such distinctions. The opinion here is that the Mets fans are missing the whole point of being worst.

Consuming with status

Holmes and I were seated tranquilly one foggy evening in his rooms in Baker Street, he swabbing his cocaine needles in blue funk and I dozing over a back issue of "Lancet," when an agitated young man burst past a protesting Mrs. Hudson and, with a beseeching gaze, cried out, "Mr. Holmes! Thank God, you're in!"

Holmes leveled him with a piercing gaze and, to my astonishment, for the fellow wore a wild expression and the most beastly provincial clothing, Holmes addressed him as though he were the oldest acquaintance in the world.

"I've been expecting you," Holmes said, pulling on his dottle. "But Holmes," I blurted, "surely . . ." "Quite right, Watson. I have never seen this young man before in my life."

"Holmes, you are amazing," I expostulated, but he no longer heard me, for he was piercing our young visitor with his steely eyes. "Come, man," he said impatiently, "get out of that foggy Burberry and sit by the fire."

Obviously puzzled by Holmes's unruffled manner, our visitor did as he was bade and when he had gotten some hot tea into him he started off more calmly. "Mr. Holmes, I need your help," he said.

87

"Quite so," said Holmes. "And I have needed yours for several weeks now. I believe the same question has had both of us puzzled. What you want to know, if I am not mistaken, is, who is the Ale Man?"

I could tell from our visitor's startled cry that Holmes had hit the mark cleanly. "But . . . but . . ." he stammered. "But how did I know?" Holmes interjected. "It was quite simple."

Holmes smiled thinly. "Amazing, Holmes, simply amazing!" I blurted. "Not at all, Watson," he said. "You see, I too have been trying for several weeks to deduce the identity of the Ale Man. Actually, the clues were too obvious. I can see that now. I made the case more difficult than it was."

"Then you know who the Ale Man is?" both the young man and myself asked in unison. "Indeed," said Holmes. "Amazing, Holmes!" I blurted. "But how did you discover it?"

"Consider what we know of the Ale Man," Holmes said. "We have seen him on television playing squash. A young man's game, squash. And yet, though young, he is affluent. After the match, remember, we see him enter a restaurant escorting a young woman dressed in Paris fashion. We see that it is an extremely expensive restaurant, of a sort that no young man can afford unless he has an expense account, has embezzled the company funds or has inherited wealth."

"Amazing, Holmes!" I blurted.

"Elementary," he murmured, tuning a violin string. "Notice, Watson, that in this expensive restaurant, he does not order either wine or spirits. He orders ale. Very revealing, that.

"We are dealing not with a man of means, but a man of beer mentality. Now we also have radio clues. In the radio commercial—surely you have heard it between innings—the Ale Man is advised by telephone that his jet to Rome is on time. He plans to leave the country. After getting his flight information, he again goes to an expensive restaurant and orders ale. Do you see the truth now, Watson?"

"God, Holmes!" I blurted, "The man is an embezzler!"

"Nonsense," he snapped. "He is none other than our

young friend here, who is also puzzled about the identity of the Ale Man."

"Amazing!" the young man blurted. "Quite," said Holmes. "Look at our young friend, Watson. What do we see? He wears a Burberry, a thornproof suit and a pair of Church's waterproof shoes. Clearly, he is an American who feels so insecure that he must advertise his taste as European. I daresay he has a Jaguar saloon garaged in Westport. This cigarette butt in his cuff shows that he has moved up to Kents. The first-class baggage tag on his greatcoat indicates that he cannot bear to travel in accommodations that persuade him to think poor."

"Do you mean—?" the young man demanded.

"I mean, sir, that *you* are the Ale Man."

"I can't believe it," the poor fellow stammered.

"Yes," said Holmes, "he's you, all right—none other than our old friend, the typical young American on the way up."

"But I never touch the stuff," the poor chap protested.

"You will now," said Holmes, "just as surely as you wear British clothing, drive a European car, fly first-class and move up from cigarette to cigarette. Would you care for more tea?"

The young man stared nervously at the pantry. "You wouldn't, by chance, have a Ballantine ale?" he asked.

"Amazing, Holmes!" I blurted.

Moving

Nobody has really done anything to solve the problem of moving since the Israelites picked up and went out of Egypt.

This country, for example, is, with the niggling exception of certain sandy sheikdoms, the most nomadic in history.

89

Each year, twenty per cent of the population moves. And yet, the science of moving here is still in the Stone Age.

We have developed mechanized farming, automated steel plants, anesthetic surgery, the automatic laundry and the electronic babysitter, but nobody is even working on a transistorized moving console. Is it simply an oversight?

The functions that such a machine ought to perform are easily defined. It should be capable of deciding which pieces of furniture are too large to negotiate the tight bend in the stairwell and advise which ones should be hoisted out of windows by pulleys. At present, millions of man-hours are lost each year getting box springs down to the stairwell bend, getting them immovably wedged, then getting them unwedged and back up the stairs to be hoisted out the window.

It must also, of course, compute the ideal location for each piece of furniture in the new house. Under the present system, months and years are wasted in shifting furniture to find the one acceptable location for each piece. No one knows how many physically unfit American men are prematurely broken by the physical labor they perform after the movers leave.

These and the other obvious mechanical functions of the moving machine surely present no challenge to American know-how. It will be more difficult to give the machine the personality necessary to make the thousands of small decisions essential to every move.

Consider the drawer problem which defeats so many moving Americans before the heavy work even begins. A successful move is an opportunity to clean up a lifetime, to cull out the junk and gew-gaws that have accumulated and made the old house a burden.

The man preparing to move begins sifting through drawers that conceal decades of indecision. The conch shell that Uncle Philip sent as a souvenir gift from Atlantic City. Those indiscreet notes lingering on from a lost youth. The moth-eaten high school letter. Match covers from New Delhi. A bag of marbles left over from school days.

Hours and days are lost reading old letters, opening old

boxes, lingering sadly over the rusting artifacts of youth. Will Uncle Philip be hurt if he learns that the conch shell is discarded? Should the high school letter be kept to remind yourself that, once, you could run 100 yards in ten seconds? Can these bits and pieces of a life be left in the trash can without creating psychic scars?

Usually, there are thousands of unmade decisions still lying about when the movers arrive, and the whole load of junk lands on the kitchen floor at the next house. A successful moving machine should be able to make these decisions painlessly, perhaps by running everything rapidly through an ingenious sorting device such as the F.B.I. uses to locate fingerprint cards.

The machine must be ruthless. It must be capable of throwing away the modeling clay and the oil paints that have been under the bed for four years waiting for someone to find time to take up the arts.

It should be particularly concerned about attics. It is a small accomplishment to have a complete thirteen-year file of New Yorker magazines stored in the attic, but the machine should be capable of insisting that it is not worth the toil of moving them across the country.

It should be merciless about throwing away the children's baby toys which parents haven't had the heart to part with, even though the dolls are armless and the rocking horse has a broken back.

It is clear that personality is the central problem in creating the ideal moving machine, for moving in the final analysis is a test of character. To know your neighbor, look at his trash on the day he moves away.

The moving machine ought to be thoroughly unpleasant, something of a Philistine, with a touch of Snopes in its character. It is not likely to be very popular, but it would take most of the misery out of moving.

91

Taxpaying

February is the time when conscientious citizens start training for the income-tax season. Such a citizen is Al Brown, thrice winner of the Internal Revenue Service's citation as Taxpayer of the Year.

Brown was interviewed recently shortly before departure for tax-training camp in Florida. He had already filed his estimated income tax form and was purring with confidence. "If I can get my eye on the old loopholes early," he said, "I ought to hit another sixty deductions with no trouble."

The new changes in the Code, he said, will make the game more wide open than ever this year. "But it just means you've got to think taxation more than ever if you want to stay out of court," he added.

At Internal Revenue, Brown is known as "The Taxpayer's Taxpayer," and no wonder. Like Rogers Hornsby, Brown refuses to read on a moving train, lest the vibration weaken the visual acuity which he brings to the depreciation table and the capital-gains clause. As the tax writers say, "He came to pay—but not very much."

What explains Brown's success? Since 1937, he has habitually read the Internal Revenue Code for two hours nightly before bed. Now near the halfway point in that fantastic instrument, he expects to finish as much as three-fourths of it before his death duties become payable.

Twice weekly, in season and out, he meets with his board of tax lawyers for lengthy speculations about the meaning of the latest Tax Court rulings. He never leaves home unaccompanied by a tax consultant to advise him how much income and what sort he can afford to accept from one hour to the next.

"It's these people who accept any income you shove at them who give the Code a bad name," Brown says. "First

92

thing they know, they're taking salary and they have to pay up, so they go around poor-mouthing the Code.

"Or they make a lot of high-surtax money writing a best-seller or winning the heavyweight championship, and the Government wants it all back. Look at Joe Louis. If he'd read his Code, he'd have gone into oil wells or bought and sold skyscrapers instead of fooling around with boxing gloves."

The secret of Brown's success is thoroughness. The upper floor of his modest two-story home is filled with filing cabinets in which every receipt he has acquired in the past three tax years is meticulously awaiting the auditor's summons.

He works there three hours each night filing the day's receipts which he collects in a large Gladstone bag as he moves about the city. "Some people say me and Alma (Mrs. Brown) have carried this thing too far," he says. "There was a lot of that talk after we had to set the bed up in the living room to make room for the gas-tax vouchers. But I tell them, 'The Code is a hard mistress.' "

Nothing irritates Brown more than modern critics who argue that the Code is hopelessly antediluvian and so complicated that nobody can understand it. These reformers argue that unless the Code is streamlined it can never hope to compete with football as a TV attraction.

"Taxpaying is the only real national pastime," says Brown. "Look at Y. A. Tittle. He's totally depleted at thirty-nine, but still has thirty or forty years of good taxpaying ahead of him. If he'd gone into taxpaying twenty years ago he would have realized there's no allowance for muscle depletion and spent his time cultivating some fast-depreciation factory machines."

"Al Brown's fidelity to the Code is a model of citizenship," comments an Internal Revenue spokesman. "Fortunately for the country, he has few imitators outside the upper brackets."

V

Fantasies for the Washington-Baffled

Why Columbus sells pizza

When Christopher Columbus first turned up in Washington seeking money to finance a voyage eastward into the uncharted Atlantic, he was warmly received.

"At first," Columbus recalled the other day over a tortoni at his little pizzeria, "I was amazed and delighted. I simply appeared at the White House gate and told the guard I had to see the President to explain that the earth was round and to tell him I could open a new route to the Indies by sailing eastward."

From the memoirs, we now know that the guard's telephoned message—"there is a nut at the gate"—was accidentally transferred to the President himself. And that the President, misunderstanding the message—he thought the guard had said, "there is a voter at the gate"—rushed out to shake hands with Columbus. (It was an election year.)

"Round, eh?" the President said after Columbus had asked for three small sailing ships. "I want you to talk to my science expert." Columbus was elated, though he began to suspect that he was in over his head the following January when the President asked Congress for the now famous forty billion dollar Earth Exploration Program, which was quickly dubbed "EEP."

"All I ever wanted," Columbus explained sadly, "was three little ships—the Nina Bird, the Pinta Bird and the L.B.J. With forty billion dollars, I was in trouble right off."

Actually, Columbus's troubles had barely begun. For six months he was denied access to EEP planners because the F.B.I. denied him a security clearance on testimony of neighbors who said he was a maniac who believed the world was round.

When clearance finally came through, Columbus found his three-ships project had been scrapped in favor of a six-stage,

97

eleven-year program to begin with the launching of un-manned photographic vessels and to end with a fifty-ship fleet that would, hopefully, put the first American on the Indies.

Congressional opposition was intense. In the years of log-rolling needed to get his appropriation, Columbus found his budget skyrocketing. When Boston got the contract for the coveted EEP launching center, Florida had to be mollified with a billion-dollar contract for an EEP sail-making center. The hull-test center went to Indiana and the foc's'le-reliabil-ity testing program to Alabama.

Texas was pacified with the enormous EEP assembly center, and the contract for the simulated ocean-proving grounds was won by Nevada, where the Government built a vast desert-locked lake, complete with simulated sea mon-sters and giant wave-making machinery.

Congressmen whose states had not been cut in on EEP gravy made life miserable for Columbus. They said he was "a crackpot round worlder." They said he would have the blood of American sailing boys on his hands when his ships went beyond Bermuda and were swallowed by sea dragons.

Some said he was a wastrel budget buster who wanted to discover more countries to give foreign aid to. Well finally, as we all remember, EEP's first manned ship was launched with the entire nation watching on television and shouting "Go! Go! Go!" as it dropped over the horizon.

Old timers still remember the shudder of disappointment which ran through the TV audience when the voyage safety director was ordered to push the destruct button. Too late, it was discovered that Columbus had forgotten to integrate his crew.

The long-awaited second voyage never got away from the dock. It was struck by the maritime unions after it was dis-covered that Columbus had once navigated a scab tugboat during a harbor strike. In the long scandalous investigation which followed, Columbus admitted that he had once ac-cepted a vicuna coat from the tycoon who held the contract for EEP's simulated ocean-proving grounds.

Columbus is now an embittered, cynical pizzeria owner. "Someday, in some simple land beyond the Atlantic," he says, "someone will go to a Queen and borrow three small ships and sail west and discover this place. I'm glad it won't be me."

The guests you meet

One of Washington's biggest, but littlest known, industries is the guest-making business. It is dominated by two giants—General Guests and National Bores Inc.—which turn out a mass-produced guest model that any hostess can show a Senator without fear of humiliation.

The guest-making business had its start in the 1930's when the number of parties given here each day began to exceed the number of Washingtonians capable of eating stuffed celery without discomposure.

It was in 1935 that the late Vincent Wottle, the genius founder of General Guests, hit upon the idea of mass producing a cheap, economically dressed guest that was tough enough to stand through seven cocktail receptions a week, yet able to accelerate quickly on low-octane bourbon.

This was Wottle's famous Model B, which revolutionized Washington entertaining. You still see them around town every evening, a bit creased about the eye sockets, to be sure, but still up to wolfing two dozen boiled shrimp at the canapé table and filling up a big room.

It remained for McMaster McDoon to see the full potential of Wottle's Model B. If Wottle could make a guest for the mass market, McDoon asked, why wasn't it possible to make an entire guest list?

Hamstrung by wartime shortages, McDoon nevertheless nourished his dream until 1947, when he startled General

Guests and astounded Washington with his now famous collapsible party. Thus was born National Bores.

McDoon was interested in supplying the mass demand for cocktail-reception guests. His original model consisted of three hundred guests. Its basic ingredients remain the same today as they were nineteen years ago.

He first built in one hundred twenty mothers who revolved slowly, talking about their children's schools. He added sixty men who would go any place to have an excuse for not going home, and sixty more who would go any place to get a free sausage and whisky.

The other parts included five svelte females who looked tantalizingly interested but kept disappearing, five great bawling women wearing badges and six press agents who insisted upon introducing people who had nothing to say to each other.

The remaining parts of the party are interchangeable. For parties that are launching Presidential candidates, National Bores uses twenty politicians who spin from hand to hand pronouncing their own names, and twenty-four political experts who plant themselves and look inscrutable. For a diplomatic occasion, it can substitute playboys, pretenders, *chargés d'affaires* and so forth.

The beauty of the collapsible party is that nobody suffers. The whole crowd is collapsed after every reception and taken back to the shop for sobering up and other maintenance. It can be used indefinitely.

The host doesn't have to worry about persuading people to come to his fling, and people, after seeing the party once, know that they can stay away from all others without missing anything.

The small, custom guest-makers, which enjoyed such a boom during the New Frontier era, report that their business has become less variegated since President Johnson began setting the social pace.

There is still great demand for their ever-popular stylized dinner partners, which come in twin sets, male and female. The females are built to flank a man during a ninety-minute, sit-down dinner and persuade him in subtle ways that he is perfectly uninteresting. The males are a set of baldish guests whose conversation for ladies is limited to Scandinavian economics or military politics.

Nowadays, however, no one wants the customized, off-beat guests which went so well in New Frontier days—the professor who could joke blithely about his book's commercial failure, the balalaika strummer who sneered at your French. One custom guest-maker who had been caught with a whole line of Ivy Leaguers on his hands was so desperate to clear his stockroom that he tried to give them away.

Nobody would have them. They had all been built to tell devastating Texas jokes at the first clink of an ice cube.

V-J Day revisited

After the last gun was silenced in World War II, a man in a six-button suit and Beatle haircut appeared from a time machine one night and wandered among a barracksful of servicemen who were awaiting discharges.

"Do you understand what this war was all about?" he asked a G.I. "Sure," the G.I. said. "We fought to save the Brooklyn Dodgers, the two-pants suit, and Mom's apple pie."

"Then you have lost," said the man from the time machine. "Within twenty years, the Dodgers will be sold out to Los Angeles. The two-pants suit is even now gone from the haberdashery rack. And by the time all of you are dads, Mom's apple pie, like almost everything else Mom used to whip up in the kitchen before Pearl Harbor, will be delivered by teamsters, frozen or ready-mixed."

The men in the barracks hooted and said that if they were not so tired of fighting they would bloody the visitor's nose on account of his feminine haircut. A cynic inter-

101

rupted, however. "That Mom's apple-pie is just a crude way of saying we fought for democracy," he said. "Pure apple-sauce. Actually, we fought to save the British Empire."

"Then you have lost," said the visitor. "The British Empire will be dissolved, at American insistence, within the decade."

"You talk like a Nazi propagandist," said a sailor. "You're trying to drive a wedge between us and the British. Next you'll be trying to divide us and our great Soviet allies."

"Within five years," the visitor. said, "any of you who calls them 'our great Soviet allies' will be accused of treason."

"Throw the bum out," shouted a corporal of infantry.

"What did you fight for, corporal?" the visitor asked.

"Easy," the corporal said. "Germany had to be destroyed."

"Then you have lost," the visitor said, "for within five years, you will be paying to rebuild Germany out of your salary. For fifteen years after that America will risk new wars to help put Germany back together again."

The men laughed and laughed. "Tell us about Asia!" shouted a marine. "Yeah," said an Air Corps private, "tell us how we're all going to wind up loving the Japs and fighting the Chinese." And the barracks rocked with laughter.

"Don't tell me you fought to destroy Japan, too," the visitor said. "What else?" a sergeant asked.

"Then you have lost," said the visitor. "Within twenty years you will rebuild Japan. It will be your warmest friend in the Pacific. When your children are born, you will teach them not to say 'Japs.' You will train them to say 'our Japanese friends.' "

"That'll be the day," said a waist gunner. "The Jap bombing of Pearl Harbor will live in infamy. We've fought to guarantee that."

"Then you have lost," said the visitor. "Within twenty years you will have large unhappy children who will not remember Pearl Harbor. They will say, however, that your

102

own bombing of Hiroshima and Nagasaki were acts of infamy."

"If any of my kids ever say that," a staff sergeant said, "they get a punch in the nose. What I fought for was none of that fancy stuff—just the good old American right to beat some sense into your own kids."

"Then you have lost," said the visitor, "for within twenty years, children who don't remember a thing about your war will outnumber you in the population, and though you may punch a few it will make no difference because your legs will be shot and your wind will be gone and your stomachs will be flabby with steak and beer."

A supply clerk who had listened solemnly spoke up. "I fought to keep America the way it is," he said.

"That's right," said a Navy gunner. "I heard Jimmy Stewart say that in the movies. I fought because I didn't want anybody changing things around America."

"Then you have lost," said the visitor, "for within twenty years everything will change. Farmers will live in the cities. City people will live in the suburbs. The country will be covered with asphalt. The cities you have known will be torn down. Money will be replaced by the credit card. Major Bowes, Charlie McCarthy and The Singing Lady will disappear.

"Your children—" here he paused to display his six-button jacket, his stovepipe pants, leprechaun boots, and his seaweed hair—"will look like me."

"All right, men," roared the top sergeant, "grab the fascist rat!" The visitor disappeared under a mass of uniformed bodies. "We'd better take him up to Intelligence for interrogation," the sergeant said. "He's probably part of a die-hard Axis scheme to destroy American morale."

When the men had untangled, of course, the visitor had spun off through the time-space continuum into 1965 and was dancing the jerk at the Go Go. "Tell me, bird," he asked his partner between twitches, "did you ever hear of a two-pants suit?"

Our appreciating statesmen

Prof. Harry I. Greenfield of Queens College proposed recently that Congress give people the same kind of tax break that machinery gets.

Greenfield, an economics professor, reasons that humans depreciate with the wear and tear of age just as surely as machinery does. Therefore, he says, it is unjust to allow tax reduction for depreciating machinery without granting it for the depreciating human organism.

This is the kind of logic that irritates Congress. It is akin to the so-called Sevareid Plan, which Congress has been trying to keep discreetly under the rug for years. Under this proposal, advanced by the essayist and commentator, Eric Sevareid, Congress would grant a human-depletion allowance to match the tax breaks accorded oil wells and other mineral resources for depletion.

Sevareid contends that humans deplete just as inexorably as oil wells. Why, he asks, is the tax law more considerate of the oil well that is going to go dry some day than of the man or woman whose youth and energy are draining away with each advancing year?

What makes these proposals such nuisances for Congress is their superficially humanitarian gloss. Naturally, Congress dislikes being portrayed as an institution that thinks more of machinery and oil wells than it does of people. And, of course, it does not.

Last year, for example, Congress wrote a tax bill that showed great consideration for people—or at least for those people who know what a capital gain is or the kind of people who occasionally transact a bit of business under the palm trees.

The point, so hard to get across, is that the tax law is constantly being revised with people in mind. The tax credit for depreciating machinery, for example, is not meant to benefit machines. It is a very human thing. It is meant to help people who own machines. The depletion allowance is not a kindness for oil wells, but for humans. It is meant to make life more agreeable for humans who own oil wells.

Of course, people who know what a capital gain is and people who do business under the palm trees and people who own machines and oil wells are admittedly a small part of the population.

It is important to give these people the tax incentive which makes the whole economy zing ever upward to new peaks of achievement and lifts the well-being of the entire population along with it. Equalizing the tax breaks, as proposed by the Greenfield or the Sevareid Plan, would require radical revision of the whole revenue structure.

The harsh fact is that the Government must be financed somehow. Suppose this burden were transferred inequitably to the oil wells. The oil wells might very well sulk and sink into a depression, fail to produce and threaten to cut off campaign contributions to their Congressmen.

The result would be a threat to both economic and political stability. Oil men might quit drilling new oil wells. On the other hand, there is no demonstrable benefit to the nation in granting a depletion allowance for humans. Even without this incentive, humans are producing to excess, thus swamping the labor market with human overflow and depressing the economy.

There are also practical political reasons why human depletion allowance and depreciation credit can never get past Congress. Congress thinks it is nonsense.

In the strange world of Congress, people do not depreciate with age. They appreciate. A Congressman rarely reaches the peak of his powers until he is seventy or eighty, and the suggestion that there is another world where he would be too old at forty for a management position, too old at sixty-five to go on working, or too depleted at eighty to run a hundred-million-dollar corporation strikes him as so much folderol.

No wonder they believe in the humanity of oil wells.

105

The disposable embassy

Government officials are at the end of their patience. They say they are tired of having Embassies wrecked around the world and will retaliate if it keeps up.

The instrument of retaliation will be an exciting new cold war weapon already undergoing secret tests in Nevada. It is called the Disposable Embassy.

As the name implies, the Disposable Embassy is designed to be thrown away. It is in the great tradition of the obsolescent car, the zip-top beer can and the throwaway plate and would, therefore, be a fitting symbol of modern American life in the foreign capitals where it would be installed.

Every American mission abroad would be kept liberally supplied with the things. Immediately after each stoning, looting or burning, the used Embassy would be put in the trash and a fresh one installed in its place. Practical advantages: no more nuisances about repairs, no more tiresome demands for restitution.

The design under test in Nevada is 88 per cent plastic and goes to pieces as effortlessly as the average Christmas toy. The first test model was 100 per cent plastic, but this proved unsatisfactory in riot tests.

Rioters who volunteered for the tests complained that the building fell to pieces or melted away before they could generate any real enthusiasm for demolishing it.

To provide a more satisfying sense of destruction, the engineers have built in cheap glass windows which give a rewarding tinkle when smashed and have added quantities of old newspapers and rags to gratify the student rioter's normal yearning for a bout of arson.

Psychologists, who were deeply involved in the project, explain that an Embassy which goes flaccidly to pieces under the first matchstick or brick has the same deficiency as a pillow when it comes to gratifying the urge for violence. It

106

simply doesn't offer enough resistance to a man whose glands are in turmoil. It leaves rioters feeling frustrated and unfulfilled.

In this state of mind, they may easily turn away from the American Embassy and wreck something else—perhaps the student riot academy of their own government. As one State Department man explained, "This would be intolerable. It would infuriate the host government, which would accuse us of meddling in their internal affairs."

The question was how to build into the Disposable Embassy enough destructive satisfaction to leave a typical Indonesian or Hungarian rioter feeling that he had really done a good day's work against the United States.

This ticklish problem was solved with matchless American ingenuity. The third-floor windows, for example, are equipped with clever spring devices which, upon being struck by bricks, eject plasticene effigies of Dean Rusk, Carl Rowan and Robert S. McNamara, all suitable for easy hanging.

At the first cry of "imperialist swine!" the Embassy front door opens automatically and four life-size, hard-rubber, battery-powered mannequins dressed like American correspondents emerge on wheels for stoning.

For the more primitive countries, whose rioters may want to vent spleen by eating a flag, styrene file cabinets will contain a few frozen spun-candy replicas of Old Glory on dry ice with printed instructions for thawing and warnings against licking the ice. (The Government doesn't want any damage suits. Bad image.)

Many people here feel that the Disposable Embassy is too brutal a weapon to be used without warning. The Embassy-wrecking powers will never forgive us, these men argue, if we callously take all the meaning out of a good Embassy bash.

If we do that, they believe, nobody will ever love us.

The hands-up bomb

When the first contingent of four million Chinese walked across the border into South Vietnam with their hands up, American authorities naturally responded with jubilation.

"The Chinese seem to have seen the light," said the Secretary of Bombing. Press headlines said "Victory in Asia!" and "Chinese Chicken Out!" Advocates of the tough policy toward Chinese Communism went on television to show how hard their noses were and to congratulate themselves on producing the cold war's first total victory.

Next morning seven million Chinese marched into Seoul, Korea, with hands up and turned themselves in to American authorities. Another nine million tramped happily into Vientiane, Laos, that afternoon and demanded to be taken into American custody.

In Washington the President, attempting to moderate the rising public joy over the apparent collapse of an ugly Asian power, pointed out that Peking had still not issued an official surrender declaration or asked for terms. As the United States did not recognize Peking, he noted, it was difficult to ask its intentions since it is awkward to address a government that does not exist.

During the following week, Peking remained silent while ninety-three million Chinese arrived in Korea and Indochina with faces smiling and hands up. Aerial reconnaissance showed that roads were clogged as far inland as Changsha and Kaifeng with people waiting in line to surrender.

Within the week, Washington was confronted with the problem of quartering and feeding one hundred sixteen million Chinese whose presence was rapidly becoming a nuisance in the already overstrained nations of the Pacific littoral.

Ebullient with victory, Congress passed emergency legislation providing for moving the prisoners to the United States, where they could be shown the American way of life and have the scales of Communism lifted from their eyes.

In vetoing these bills, the President pointed out that Chinese already in hand would occupy all the territory between St. Louis and Tucson and that an appropriation of $275 billion would be needed to sustain them for one year at the prevailing American standard of living.

It was essential, he added, to determine Peking's intentions and, therefore, he had wired Peking—whether it existed or not—the following message: "If you surrender, say 'Uncle' ten times."

Meanwhile, the National Security Council, having scented a crisis, was in continuous session with hawks and doves at each other's throat feathers. General d'Arcy Freeblood (U.S.A., retired), the nationally syndicated hawk whose calls for total victory had terrified thirty million breakfast readers daily ever since Chiang had fled the mainland, was the first to note the peril for the public.

"Unless the Chinese surrender rate abates suddenly and dramatically," he wrote, "we will have more Chinese than Americans on our hands within the next six days. The ugly fact is that we have been the victims of surprise surrender. The President must screw up his courage and warn Peking that we will not take total Chinese surrender lying down."

Then came the President's magnanimous gesture to Peking. "If you will surrender decently—which is to say, give up and keep your people to yourself—you will never regret it," he declared.

In the American tradition, he proposed to do for China what had been done for Germany and Japan after their surrenders in 1945. Within twenty years, he pledged, China would live in velvet. Its factories would boom. It would have a magnificent system of *rickshabahns* and every Chinese would have a Volkswagen and be able to vacation in Italy.

"When we have finished putting China on its feet," he promised, "the yuan will be stronger than the dollar, and China will be able to take out of Fort Knox whatever gold

109

has not already been claimed by the defeated powers of World War II."

Peking said nothing, but India, Brazil and Great Britain immediately replied that they were ready to surrender on the President's terms. Their offers were curtly rejected as unworthy of friendly governments.

Finally, with Chinese surrenders mounting, the President announced his historic pre-emptive no-win policy. "China has undertaken to destroy us with a population bomb dropped upon us with its hands up," the prologue began. "By surrendering four hundred million people, it can increase our tax burden, overcrowd our classrooms, empty our supermarket shelves and paralyze traffic."

Chinese surrender had to be stopped at any cost, he said. "Our policy must be unremitting antagonism—an antagonism that must never be permitted to end in victory for us. By refusing to settle for victory, we will assure that the Chinese can never triumph."

And finally, the military heart of pre-emptive no-win: "If China, ever again, attempts another of these surrenders anywhere in Asia, we will bomb her until she stops it."

As General Freeblood later conceded, "It isn't really peace, of course, but the beauty of pre-emptive no-win is that we will never have to think about the terrible problem that would result from total victory. That way, war is more fun."

Inside the cocktail circuit

So many people have demanded to know what excesses go on in Washington after dark that it has been necessary to retain the notorious double agent, Otto Upjohn, to infiltrate and report on a typical Washington reception. His report follows:

After closing eyes and choosing at random from a list of twenty-three crashable receptions being held on a typical night last week, I appeared at the new Madison Hotel's press reception to celebrate its opening. Decorously attired ("In deference to the sensibilities of its patrons, the management of the Madison reserves the right to insist that its guests be decorously attired," the press notices had cautioned) I proceeded to the mezzanine trying to look as much as possible like the press.

Following ears towards source of noise, sighted fifty or sixty people crushing each other at entrance to a black-ceilinged, oblong cavern. Progress barred by nervous-looking fellow, obviously a public-relations man on lookout for famous press personalities and off-duty bellboys in mufti trying to sneak a free martini.

"Upjohn of The Times," I said. "Glad you could make it, Mr. Ugstein," he said, inviting me to sign guest book and introducing himself by name that sounded like "Brrmm Shhrrmmn."

Two things immediately became obvious: 1—Task of keeping off-duty bellboys from crashing typical Washington reception is impossible; 2—Everybody you meet at typical Washington reception is named "Brrmm Shhrrmmn."

Found myself in tow behind second public-relations man determined to introduce me to a public-relations man who would introduce me to Suzy Parker, actress, model, "press hostess" for evening. Bulled our way through mob jamming entrance to oblong cavern. Very dark inside. Sense of suffocation intense among masses of dimly seen bodies milling in search of bar. Very difficult to breathe due to dense layers of cigarette smoke.

Introduced to third public-relations man. "Mr. Brrmm Shhrrmmn, this is Mr. Otterbein of Time. Introduce him to our press hostess."

Asked Brrmm Shhrrmmn what a "press hostess" did. "Who knows?" he shrugged. "They come here and they stand around like this." Asked him why Miss Parker had chosen to be "press hostess" for the Madison. Brrmm Shrrmmn

111

laughed and laughed. "I paid her a thousand bucks and she came down here. That's why," he said.

"Suzy, Suzy!" Brrmm Shhrrmmn said, "Meet Mr. Woodbine of Time." Found myself eyeball to eyeball with tall, handsome redhead wearing golden hostess gown said to have been modeled on a Dolley Madison original. "This is the closest Dolley Madison gown we could get," said Brrmm Shhrrmmn. "Cost us five hundred bucks at Bonwit Teller."

Confronted by beautiful woman, I yielded to impulse to make clever conversation. Asked Suzy if she felt more chic wearing Dolley Madison gown·than she did in Diors or Balenciagas. "This is a hostess gown that's meant to be worn at home," she said, "and in this crowd people keep stepping on it."

"Hurry him up," somebody said to Brrmm Shhrrmmn. "Earl Warren is waiting to meet her." Noted Chief Justice and Mrs. Warren gazing approvingly at Suzy. Determined not to yield position to big names.

"Suzy, Suzy! Buchwald is here!" panicked public-relations man shouted. Pandemonium. Miss Parker swept away from me and Chief Justice. Battalion of photographers flashing bulbs at her greeting fellow named Buchwald. Apparently a relative of Madison owners.

Someone introduced me to Enrico Caruso, New York hairdresser who did Miss Parker's hair in Dolley Madison style after studying painting of Dolley. Asked price of hairdo. "For a cut and set—$25," Caruso said. Interview also adduced that Caruso is not related to the singing Enrico Caruso, speaks no Italian, and gets airsick when forced to fly.

Drifted into dense mass to see what other celebrities present besides Warren. Noted several familiar press people, attired none too decorously, but no celebrities. Most of guests may have been off-duty bellboys and girl friends.

Let myself float on human tide to catch mood of reception. Many people saying, "That's Suzy. Have you met Suzy?" Others exchanging introductions: "Have you met the Brrmm Shhrrmmns?" Others asking direction to bar. Usual buffet—

shrimp and canapes—hidden behind wall of people five deep.

Suddenly felt alienated, lonely, hungry, in need of a drink, full of strangers' cigarette smoke. Same symptoms I experienced when last attended typical Washington reception several years ago.

Sad to reflect on thousands of people all over town attending typical Washington receptions every night.

The Fort Knox caper

Agent Bix Stover, Yale '61, *persona non grata* Moscow '63, has turned in his snub-nosed Beretta at C.I.A. and vanished into the trackless wastes of his father's department-store chain.

Stover, the story goes, was summoned recently into the presence of his chief and asked if he was fit to take on an extraordinary assignment. Always keen for adventure, Stover declared himself ready to go.

Quickly, with customary economy of speech, the chief laid the puzzle in Stover's lap. "What we are up against," he explained, "is nothing less than a plot to strip Fort Knox down to its last gold brick."

Behind the scheme, he went on, loomed the mysterious Frenchman, Charles deGaullefinger, whose soubriquet, "The Man of Destiny," sent shudders through the Anglo-Saxon chanceries of the world. Already, Fort Knox was down to its last $15 billion in bullion. Such large quantities of gold had turned up in Paris that Frenchmen would no longer sell an American the Eiffel Tower for paper dollars.

"And you want me to track down this deGaullefinger, lure him into a game of high-stakes blackjack and win back the gold," Stover said. "Nonsense, Stover," the chief snapped. "I want you to find out how the fellow does it."

113

The chief became confidential. The galling thing about deGaullefinger, he explained, was that his methods seemed perfectly legal. There was no official disposition to proceed against him at the card table.

"You see, Stover, the man is operating through the international monetary system."

"Devilish," said Stover.

"Yes," said the chief, "isn't it?"

There was a long, uneasy pause, broken finally when Stover confessed, "Sir, I'm afraid I don't know anything about the international monetary system."

"That's what makes it so cunning, Stover. Neither does anyone else. You see the point?"

"I am to find out how the international monetary system works?"

"Exactly. My wife and I are having guests to dinner next week. The only topic of conversation in Washington is the balance of payments deficit, the gold drain, the loss of confidence in the dollar, and deGaullefinger. I want to sit down at that dinner prepared to talk international money."

For ten days, Stover moved among the nation's canniest bankers and economists. "The public doesn't understand the seriousness of the money crisis," they told him happily.

"Explain it to me," he said. They laughed in his face. They explained that it was foolish for anybody but a banker or an economist to try to understand international money matters.

He asked two of the most brilliant economists on earth why gold was so important. "It isn't," said one. "It is, too," snarled the other.

"Gold has nothing to do with it," a shrewd banker told him. "It is a question of confidence. Psychological, you see." Stover decided to test the psychological-depression theory of money. At lunch, he watched five bankers slowly losing confidence in the dollar and spiked their coffee with pep pills. Next day they reported they had lost more confidence than ever.

Next, Stover spent two days investigating his own household. There, he discovered to his amazement, nobody had lost the slightest bit of confidence in the dollar. His wife still wanted every dollar he could find. His child wanted a dollar. The mail was full of notices from merchants who wanted dollars.

When his butter-and-egg man demanded eight dollars, Stover asked him why the gold drain had not shaken his confidence in the dollar. The butter-and-egg man sneered at him. "You talk like one of those nut bankers in Switzerland," he said. "You want I should take payment in piasters?"

Stover went to the Secretary of Clarification. "Europe is losing confidence in the dollar, but my butter-and-egg man isn't," he said. "Naturally," said the Secretary, "the butter-and-egg man is concerned with real wealth, which has never been greater in this country. Europe is concerned with little men in Zurich, who are concerned with the balance of payments graph, which has never been poorer.

"If the little men in Zurich think the little men in Paris are afraid that little men in Milan will be depressed by the balance of payments graph, we have a crisis of confidence, you see."

Finally Stover reported to his chief. "There is an international monetary system, all right," he wrote, "but bankers and economists don't understand it either. For dinner conversation, suggest you say so and urge creation of a common-sense system."

The chief called for Stover's resignation next day. "Anybody who thinks you can stop deGaullefinger with common sense has no place in the United States Government," he said.

115

VII

The Tic Generation

The disposable man

How far is American know-how from producing a disposable man?

Closer perhaps than it seems. Sears, Roebuck and Company is already marketing a stingless bee, for people who want to keep bees without really being bothered. The stingless bee, of course, was inevitable, just as the disposable man is. It is merely the latest in a long line of technological breakthroughs that have brought us into the Nothing Generation or, as social psychologists might call it, the Non Age.

The purpose of the Non Age is to make it possible for the Nothing Generation to get through a complete non-life without any of the untidy bothers of living, like bee stings. Hence, the non-bee.

Other adjuncts of the good non-life include the fuzzless peach, the seedless grape, and odorless booze (vodka). All serve the same basic function as the stingless bee. They relieve man of the need to come to grips with nature by devising schemes to keep peach fuzz off his chin, seeds out of his appendix and neighbors from knowing that he is snockered.

The child of the Nothing Generation is naturally swaddled in a disposable diaper. As he grows he goes to the painless dentist. His father lives in a no-down-payment house and wears a wrinkle-free, drip-dry wardrobe. On formal occasions, he wears a clip-on tie.

The essence of non-life is non-involvement, more positively known as playing it safe. And so literature has created the anti-hero for the anti-theater and the anti-novel. The anti-hero sits around in garbage cans doing nothing for hours, except saying "no" to life and waiting to be disposed of. He is a great favorite of the Nothing Generation, which can listen to him for hours, even on caffeine-free coffee.

When the anti-hero wants to carbonate his stomach he takes a non-caloric soft drink. It comes in a disposable, no-deposit no-return bottle, or a throwaway can. For amusement he sits in dehumidified air watching non-actors perform non-dramas about non-people and absorbing advertisements that tell how to take the misery out of washday, the odors out of living and the challenge out of opening a milk can.

The beauty of the Non Age is that it makes non-life so easy, and creates so much leisure time to enjoy non-living. The disposable diaper, for example, not only takes half the agony out of parenthood, but also gives the parents time to drink more odorless booze, without offending baby's delicate nose.

The throwaway bottle saves them from the unpleasantness of seeing junior sulk when ordered to take the bottles back to the store. It also gives them a chance to worry each other about why junior has nothing to do with his time but wolf fuzzless peaches and seedless grapes.

The Non Age, fortunately, provides for junior, should the non-life hang heavily on his hands and make him edgy. The doctor will prescribe some tranquillizers to keep him in a non-emotional state. The prescription will be written with a throwaway pen.

In this state junior may be induced to turn down the anti-music on the phonograph and turn his hand to something perfectly unchallenging, like keeping stingless bees.

The stingless bee, incidentally, reached the market at the same time as the topless bathing suit and the topless evening gown, which had just appeared in London. Both will soon take the last disturbing shred of curiosity out of anti-hero.

What next in the march toward a better non-life for all Americans? The workless job is already well developed. The disposable conscience is old hat. There is room perhaps, as recent events in the old South suggest, for the painless truncheon, though a case can be made that when safe, uninvolved non-living becomes absolute, everything will be painless.

No. What the Nothing Generation needs for self-completion is the disposable man. He will be able to pass from disposable diaper to the trash can, leaving no trace but an irrevocable trust for his disposable children.

Hints for teens

Instructions for teen-agers:

1. Always leave the shoes in the center of the living-room floor where the parents will be certain to notice them. Let the parents call you three times to come pick up the shoes before you hear them. Then say, "Were you calling *me?*"

After a few months the parents will pick up the shoes themselves, reasoning that this is easier than shouting your name four times. Once the parent is conditioned to picking up the shoes without making a scene, he will naturally take on other housekeeping chores connected with your presence and cease harassing you to pick up skirts left under your bed, soda pop bottles left in the shower stall, bicycle chains left on the refrigerator, etc.

2. Use the record player at all times while in the house. Acquire no more than six records and play them at peak volume, starting immediately after entering the house and leaving the shoes in the living room.

In a short while the parents will stop saying, "No!" when you ask permission to go out. If dealing with unusually obdurate parents, have three or four friends drop by and bring their records just before the hour when the parents normally sit down to watch Lawrence Welk or to read "The Decline and Fall of the Roman Empire."

3. Arrange to have fifteen or twenty friends telephone you at five-minute intervals at all times while you are out of the house. The parents will eventually tire of answering the phone and come to realize that the phone belongs to you. Thereafter they will be apologetic about asking to use the phone when you are using it to play your record collection to your best friend.

4. When ordered to bathe, always take the best towels. Do not bathe too thoroughly, but merely wet the body enough to produce muddy rivulets in its creases. Use the best towels

121

to remove the streaks. Then splash water over the bathroom floor and mop it with the towels. Throw the towels under your bed. In due time, the parents will become less insistent about forcing you to bathe when you would prefer to listen to the top forty.

5. Never hide the cigarettes in the kind of places parents use to hide things. You will know from experience what places these are.

6. When using the parents' car, never practice a racing getaway until you are two blocks from the house.

7. After using the parent's necktie or hosiery, remove it and leave it in the dog's or the cat's favorite sleeping place. This will assure you a fashionable wardrobe turnover to keep you in the style forefront of your group.

8. When in need of money, be helpful around the house. Insist upon making breakfast, taking pains to burn the bacon and overcook the coffee. Go off without fanfare and clean your room, being certain to splash the floor wax over the bedspread. When the parents tax you with incompetence, assume an expression of contrite misery while explaining that they have never given you the opportunity to assume the responsibility of being self-reliant.

If they obtusely miss the point and withhold the money, make the parents feel guilty by reminding them that it was their generation that produced the atomic bomb.

9. Invent another set of parents. Attribute them to Joe or Angela. When the parents are intolerable, tell them things such as, "Angela's parents are letting *her* stay out until midnight," and "Gosh, Joe's parents don't care if *he* has a beer once in a while."

In all cases, the invented set of parents must be shown to have the teen-age spirit. At dinner, for example, it is effective to say, "Gee, Angela's parents listen to the Beatles all day long!" Being compared to Angela's parents will eventually make other parents feel very old and broken in spirit.

In this condition, it is a small task to reduce them to complete surrender.

All downhill from Babylon

Fashion has rarely been more cruel to girls than it is right now. It is sad watching them struggle to cope with the dangerous-woman costume that style has clamped upon them.

When the offices empty at lunchtime, they flock out wearing their Theda Bara eyes, their metallic hair and their diamondback-rattler hose, and the effect is enough to make a man think of seraglios, penthouse midnights by candlelight and wrecked homes. Then they all go to the drugstore fountain and eat hamburgers and milkshakes.

This is bound to place intolerable psychic strains on a girl. She is dressed to feel dangerous, perfumed to exude suggestions of nights in Babylon, and painted to drive men insane. How can she possibly avoid facing up to the terrible chasm between dream and reality when, in this musky state of mind, she must sit at a formica bar and squeeze mustard out of a plastic bottle?

The terrible truth, which must be apparent at moments like this, is that she has neither the resources nor the disposition to make a success of dangerous living. She is fated to wind up with her hair in curlers driving a prosaic baby to the supermarket in a station wagon.

In the evenings when the man she has trapped with exudations of Babylon arrives home to find her frying liver and potatoes, there will be unpleasant little conversations. "Not feeling dangerous tonight, I see." "Oh, it's you." "I'm afraid it is." And so forth.

The trouble here is that the girl has been as badly betrayed as the boy by the fashion setters. As the population explosion since World War II attests, what she truly wants of life is not a sultry gambol in the seraglio but the chance to fry liver in a mortgaged ranch house.

By dressing her in the delusion that she can have both,

123

fashion plays her a cruel and possibly a home-wrecking blow, as both boy and girl begin to fret about missing out on the promise of dangerous living.

The current fashion in dancing is creating another kind of confusion that is quite different but no less evil for the girls. The new dancing, as exemplified by the watusi, the frug and the monkey, is leading the girls into a totally fallacious theory of the dance. It is a pathetic sight to watch them at it, bucking, heaving and twitching like so many poor beasts being tormented with electric cattle prods.

The father of these dances is not "Killer Joe" Piro, society's dance teacher, as widely reported, but Max Cohen, a strip-tease impresario who ran the celebrated Oasis Club in Baltimore during the 1930's and early 1940's.

Max's boast was that he offered "the worst show in town." His secret was to let any waitress who was so disposed step into the spotlight and try to do a strip tease. It was terrible. The poor girls would fling themselves around, bucking, heaving and twitching, while the audience went wild with laughter.

What those girls were doing was what we now call the watusi, the frug and the monkey. Once they learned to do a passable strip tease, they moved on to the clubs that were trafficking in lust, for Max's formula called for low comedy.

Now that his dances have become fashionable, the sweetest, loveliest girls in the country are being conditioned to think of dancing as basically absurd. All over the country there are girls who sincerely believe that fun is like being electrified with a cattle prod while their men imitate waitresses trying their first striptease.

In a few years these poor girls will thicken in the waist and calcify in the lumbar and need to be held tenderly and guided slowly around the dance floor in the arms of men who will love them despite their loss of elasticity.

Even if a few men with such skills survive, the girls will feel that time has cut off their fun just as cruelly as marriage has shackled them to fried liver. Yes, it is sad.

Therapy in parachute

Dr. Harold Liverworth, writing in his syndicated column, "Aches and Pains," is exhilarated by the spreading popularity of skydiving. He recommends it to the middle-aged for its excellent stretching action on the spine, but believes that it offers unique therapeutic values for unhappy adolescents. If developed under responsible community supervision, Dr. Liverworth asserts, skydiving can become a healthy acceptable substitute for such antisocial youth pastimes as "chicken," tire-slashing and putting detergent into public fountains.

Skydiving, for the benefit of those still unaware of this newest of sports, consists of leaping from an airplane and falling at speeds of from one hundred twenty to one hundred and eighty miles an hour (depending on the diver's attitude) toward the earth. Few activities more nearly satisfy the youthful craving for "kicks," Dr. Liverworth writes, particularly in the case of a dive without parachute.

In this maneuver, the object is to receive a chute from a fellow falling nearby (considerable lateral movement is possible in a skillful free fall) and to get the thing attached to the body and opened before one reaches the earth. The doctor cautions, however, that anyone expecting to enjoy this sort of sport on his first few jumps is approaching skydiving in the wrong frame of mind and should consult his family physician.

In the elementary stages, the skydiver learns to fall a mile or two with chute unopened, then to steer himself onto small bull's-eyes on the ground. Dr. Liverworth sees the act of free fall as a sublimation of modern youth's hatred and repressed urge to destroy a disordered world.

"In free fall, for a minute or so, the young diver escapes the terrible society where the bomb threatens constantly to destroy him," the doctor writes. "He is himself the bomb,

125

venting his awful energies on a world he despises. The jump, if successfully completed, cleanses him of impulse to release his obsessions in petty acts such as party-crashing and tearing up boardwalk beano parlors."

Unfortunately, many persons have a primitive fear of high places which will preclude skydiving's becoming the cure-all for modern adolescent neurosis. Some of the benefits, however, can still be obtained, Dr. Liverworth suggests, if parents will rig a simple chest-and-hip harness and pulley in the stairwell or garage rafters.

The hostile teen-ager may then be hoisted into the free-fall position—that is, spread-eagled face down—and encouraged to fancy himself a bomb hovering over his parents. The doctor gives stern warning, however, against leaving the youth suspended once he insists on being let down.

Dr. Liverworth's optimistic view that youth can be successfully integrated into society comes as a great comfort after the depressing pronouncements by Life and Look that today's young are a hopeless case.

The doctor thinks Life went badly wrong in suggesting that off-duty policemen be engaged to keep order when planning a teen-agers' party in the home. He deems it weak psychology to let the youngsters feel they are not trustworthy.

His sensible advice for parents who simply must have teen-agers' parties in the home is to take any unpleasant party-crasher aside and explain to him in a rational manner that what he really wants to destroy is not this particular house, but the whole impossible world.

This can be touchy—some of these brutes are mountainous at seventeen nowadays—but if carried off with finesse, it should be an easy matter to get the poor boy up in the stairwell skydiving harness, where he will either sublimate his aggressions peacefully or sleep it off. At least, that's what Dr. Liverworth maintains.

Mike

Soliloquy for 9-year-olds on Report-Card Day:
"My name is Mike. I'm a kid. A kid is somebody who
when you want to go out and play kick-the-can has got to sit
in a dull old schoolroom all day because his Daddy wants
him to get into Yale instead of hanging around the filling
station all the time when he grows up.

"My teacher is Miss Plover. She is all right except she is
wrinkled and don't like it when you hit the girls too hard in
dodge ball and don't do your homework on time. Miss Plover
she gave us these report cards today. I think she's crazy or
something.

"I mean, all the marks are just the same as last time. All
C's. Except on work and study habits which she only give me
a D on, and last time I got a C. Man, it's tough being a kid
when you got a hard marker like Miss Plover and have got to
take home a report card like this.

"Last night Daddy was feeling good and said how I was
going to get a better report card this time because he cut
out a lot of television and put on the pressure, you know.

"I think he meant, you know, how he'd been making me
go up to my room every night and read this terrible book
where some guy named Ulysses is supposed to be sailing
around in a boat trying to get into Yale or something. It's
called the Odyssey or the Idiocy and Mom says it's too old
for a kid, but Dad says he read in Life magazine how they
put kids under this awful pressure at Yale and the sooner I
get used to it the better.

"Anyhow, it makes a kid want to cry when you think of
having to show Mom and Dad a report card like this. It's like
the pressure didn't do any good at all with Miss Plover, but I
can't help it if Miss Plover just doesn't like me, can I?

"I mean, how come she's always giving that Linda Lee
Lackenbush A's just because she's always jumping up and

127

waving her hand because she knows who wrote Peter Rabbit and how much four times eight is and nobody ever asks me a question except when I been looking out the window or thinking about Superman? You got to be a girl to get a good mark off Miss Plover.

"I bet Linda Lee Lackenbush don't know the Beatles from the Animals. That's the kind of kid Miss Plover likes. I wouldn't mind too much only except for Communism.

"Communism is where they're putting this awful pressure on all the kids so they can get to the moon and all sit around telling each other how much nine times eight is and laughing because Yale didn't cook up enough pressure to get its men there first.

"I heard all about it on the transistor one night. You see, I got this transistor I put under the blanket and listen to the Animal Hour on every night when I'm reading the Idiocy. This man comes on for two minutes and tells how Communism is making all its kids miserable so they can get to the moon.

"Then he says that any of us kids that can't take the pressure are letting the country down and got to get out of the way for kids like Linda Lee Lackenbush who got the stuff to get into Yale and keep the country from being laughed at from the moon.

"Then he turns real mean about us other kids and says we're all going to wind up like bums. It makes you think.

"I'd like to go to the moon some time. I heard it's cool, only it wouldn't be much fun if you're with a bunch of girls like Miss Plover gives the A's to. They'd just sit around bragging about Yale.

"Maybe if I cry when I get home Dad won't be so sore. I bet it wasn't this lousy being a kid in his days."

Barney (Mike ten years after)

American youth is confused. It cannot get the point of what American life is all about. A tragic example is a lad named Barney, who has just been haled before the Council of Elders again for admonitory lecturing on the American way.

Several years ago Barney was at State University, majoring happily in football weekend, fraternity science and the philosophy of the convertible coupe. One day the Russians placed a piece of metal in orbit around the earth, and Barney was summoned before the Council of Elders.

"You are letting America down," the Elders said. "How do you think this country can survive if you are content to loaf while Russians spin metal through the ionosphere?"

The chastened Barney quit his fraternity, started hissing the football team and grew wan and spooky as he mastered the conjugation of Greek verbs, the melting point of vanadium, the categorical imperative and the far outposts of biochemistry. In no time at all he was back before the Elders.

"Look at yourself," they said. "You are a colorless drone. What this country needs is not a mass of young bookworms, but well-rounded mature citizens who know how to live the well-balanced life. Along with your studies, you must learn how to relax and get more out of living."

Accordingly, when Easter recess came, Barney obediently went to Fort Lauderdale and had a wonderful time tearing up the town. That summer he went to the Newport Jazz Festival and tore up Newport.

"Barney," said the Great Elder, "you have to understand that these violent outbursts are sick and antisocial. What this country needs is young people who will leave college prepared to fit into society and make a positive constructive contribution."

For a year Barney studied American society and prepared

129

himself to fit in. He bought an Ivy League wardrobe, insured himself heavily and started angling for a job that would allow him to retire at forty-five with a comfortable annuity. Whenever politics was discussed, he said that politics was not up his alley, and whenever anybody made a slighting remark about the Government, he made a note of it in his diary against the possibility that he might someday be interrogated by the F.B.I.

"It won't do, Barney," the Elders told him. "You're too cautious, too conformist, too security minded. What America needs is youth with the courage to be different."

Depressed but still loyal, Barney transferred to the University of California, where he grew a beard, began speaking well of Mao Tse-tung and agitating for free speech. In six weeks he was back before the Council.

"When we urged you to have the courage to be different," the Great Elder explained with infinite patience, "we did not mean the courage to be terribly different."

While free speech was all right in its place, the Great Elder went on, Mao was distinctly outside the American mainstream. "Stay between Norman Thomas and Barry Goldwater," he advised. "Find something typically American and get committed to it. This country needs a youth that is more vitally committed."

Finally, still in his beard, Barney took part in a civil rights sit-in protesting in a generalized way against the theory that people who want to vote ought to be clubbed by the police. His appearance before the Elders was more argumentative than usual.

While it was certainly unjust to club persons for wanting to vote, the Elders explained, the American way was to rely on the law. By engaging in a sit-in, Barney had violated the law. In its way, sitting-in was as dangerous to American life as the beating of people who wanted to vote and, indeed, the punishment was usually more severe.

For the first time in all his hearings, Barney spoke. "I must be growing up," he said, "for I think I understand. You are

130

saying that sitting-in is just as bad as blowing up Sunday schools."

"Ah," said the Great Elder with infinite sadness, "when you are truly grown up you will learn not to give such emotional interpretations to the wisdom of your Elders." He paused a moment. "Why don't you get committed to something that people don't care about so much?" he suggested. "That's the kind of commitment this country expects of its youth."

Adieu, Old Mr. Muscles

Magazines like Harper's Bazaar are the poor man's LSD. For a mere seventy-five cents, they give you two hundred and fifty lotus leaves which, if chewed slowly in a lavender room and washed down with large draughts of beer, induce hallucinations that make the peyote chewer's seem, by contrast, as bland as a Juicy Fruit hangover.

The addict seizes his Vogue or Bazaar from his mailman connection, dashes to his cork-lined room, sinks to a bombazine chaise longue and mainlines it in both eyeballs, passing quickly from agitation to wild hallucination into deep stupor.

The April 1965 issue of Harper's Bazaar, where this young male aberration first appeared, seemed at first to be nothing stronger than the usual rich dose with its lush, vision-inducing portraits of a life so outrageously chic, so gay, so fey, so exclusive that ten minutes exposure to it often produces a fatal giddiness.

There were the usual pictures of adorable doe-eyed young men fresh from the most frightfully modish pastimes. ("A familiar figure at Happenings, gallery openings, Underground movies and dinner parties, he is persistently on the scene, dead-center in the concentric circles of New York.")

There was the usual fun advice on shedding weight.

131

("Frug that fat away.") And our old friend, Stunningly Elegant New Common Market Duchessa. ("Ineffable elegance, an aristocracy of being that transcends the illusory in fashion, simply, unself-consciously exists.")
There were the models wearing women's clothes. . . . Where do they get those models? Somebody must build them out of Tinker Toys. They become more sinister as the clothes they model become more blatantly expressive of their designers' distaste for women. Any month now they may all turn up carrying whips.
Leafing drunkenly from page to page brought on the fantasies in full strength. Going, going, going, gone, and there you are frugging that fat away in a London club so exclusive that only Princess Margaret, Baby Jane Holzer, Vidal Sassoon and Nureyev are permitted to stare.
A ravishing Duchessa who simply, unselfconsciously exists is carefully, with the aid of surveyors, adjusting her chair to dead center of New York concentric circles, and you spiral down into that ineffable slumber in which there is no reality.
And then, a terrible jarring return to consciousness as the mind laps up a piece of small print. Its subject: Frankly Beautiful New Young Gentleman. "Say it ain't so, Harper's Bazaar," the addict wants to sob, as he reads on and on about Frankly Beautiful New Young Gentleman with his "long, extremely tossable hair," always simply, unselfconsciously existing "wherever the action is in the space age world of now."
F.B.N.Y.G., say the editors, makes "Old Mr. Muscles" look "as square and wiped-out as the Hupmobile." Girls adore him, particularly for his "consummate cool." They are excited by the fact that "he brushes his hair with absorption, chooses his shampoos with the gravity of a connoisseur, and scents himself with enormous care." Which is not the worst of it.
He "seriously collects colognes, perfumes, powders, shave creams and shampoos. Tomorrow, almost surely, he will order unguents for his complexion, masks for his circulation and—who knows?—make-up for his . . . beauty."

At this pause in the prose, most addicts are about to tell Harper's Bazaar that Frankly Beautiful New Young Gentleman had better not come calling on their daughters, or their sons either, with his tossable hair, carefully scented pelt and complexion unguents.

Harper's Bazaar has a curt answer: "How you feel about this frankly beautiful new young gentleman is, frankly, your own business. But this much is certain. You must reckon with him. He is here—and now."

The first impulse is irrational: Reckon with him, eh? How about a punch in the nose for openers? Then, the awful self-discovery: This is the Old Mr. Muscles mentality at work; merely suggesting it makes a man look as square and wiped-out as the Hupmobile.

The trap is sprung. Frankly Beautiful New Young Gentleman is too bad, but not as bad as feeling square and wiped-out. To be with it people will do anything, including swallowing live goldfish. By planting the idea that among the modern young, feminine is masculine, Harper's Bazaar leaves millions of aging American male youthomaniacs no alternative but the cultivation of tossable hair and appointments at the beauty salon.

Old Mr. Muscles? Not dad, son. He'd rather be caught choosing his perfume like a connoisseur. . . .

There are consolations. The clothes those fashion models wear can finally be worn by men, for whom they seem to be designed anyhow. And it may very well end the population explosion.

Little Klaus, please. . . .

An all-purpose Father's Day message to middle-class children:

The presents were fine. Just what Daddy wanted. A fifth of bay rum, a Beatles record, the new edition of Mad magazine and Senator Goldwater's "The Conscience of a Conservative." As Daddy is sleeping late this morning, will you please play the Beatles record in the cellar until you hear Mr. Brown next door start his power mower?

Daddy would also like to pass up breakfast in bed this year. He has always wondered how Gloria Swanson managed to eat all those breakfasts in bed without getting butter on the pillows. Besides, no matter what you think, Daddy is still too young to start eating in bed.

On this day when you are all· thinking of your father's happiness, you may want to know what you can do to make him—and Mommy too—feel like better parents. Please accept what Dad is going to tell you here in the spirit of love because he doesn't want you to grow up and have to go to a psychiatrist.

First of all, little Klaus: You have been smoking again. It's no use denying it because Daddy found the butts in the garage yesterday. And, incidentally, he also found those two copies of Playboy hidden under the woodpile. Nine is too young to start smoking. Daddy realizes that with all the anxiety about the bomb and the mess the world's in, childhood isn't easy any more, but he doesn't like to think of you being rejected by the draft for emphysema, or something even worse, when you are only nineteen.

And you, Norris, you could make your father a happier man if you would take the matches away from Klaus when you see him lighting up. Mother is certain that you are the one who took "Tropic of Cancer" from Daddy's bottom drawer. Daddy doesn't want to be priggish. He knows that with television and the Supreme Court, children are exposed to a lot more nowadays than they used to be.

Still, at twelve, if you can read Henry Miller, you ought to be able to read "Tom Sawyer" too. Dad realizes that reading can be a drag—between us, he cut his wisdom teeth on "Spicy Adventure"—but it was easier to get into a prestige college in those days.

Now Dad doesn't want to give you college neurosis by pressuring you to think about Harvard while you are still in the seventh grade, but the fact is, if you don't buckle down to "Tom Sawyer," Harvard isn't going to take you, and then you're not going to be able to get into one of the big corporations and have your own Ferrari when you grow up.

Sweet Hedvig, what a big girl you are getting to be! But darling, you are still only a teen-ager, and it would make Dad so much happier if you would come in nights before he goes to bed.

It would also be nice if you would quit riding with that young Erwin. He not only drives like a maniac, but he throws beer cans all over the neighborhood. How nice it would be if you could spend a little time with the Carrothers boy, who has been accepted at M.I.T. These gadget-minded boys will own the world by 1984.

Now, from all of you, what Dad would like most is a little more sense of responsibility. At your ages, there is no reason why you have to be driven four blocks to the grocery when you want soda pop. When your father was a child—. Well, never mind that.

The important thing is that you all find something rewarding and satisfying to do with your lives. Do you want to grow up without a Harvard diploma and with emphysema and with white backlash? Or do you want to do better than your parents have done?

Do you want to become the kind of parents who, on Father's Day or Mother's Day, have nothing inspirational to tell their children? If so, keep up the smoking and forget about Harvard and keep riding around with that young Erwin.

Daddy works hard to give you everything you want. In return, if in spite of him things turn out well, will you please have the grace not to recall how badly he managed fatherhood?

Dad tyrannized

A man who spends a good bit of time idling in supermarkets submits the following commentary on the decline of an honored American industry:

"This occurred to me suddenly the other day while I was studying life in a mammoth new supermarket near my home. I had only been to this particular supermarket three or four times before, and had found it pretentious, dull and poorly organized. It takes a good fifty-yard walk, for example, to get from the imported English soda crackers to the domestic cracker shelf, and for some reason pickles have been located a half block away from the martini olives.

"My chief objection to it, however, is that the customers seem to be ill at ease and on guard. The pleasure of supermarket idling lies in watching people with their hair down— or, in the case of the women, up.

"But I'm dawdling. The point is that this particular supermarket, located in an upper middle-class neighborhood, seemed to put people on guard. Before Christmas, for example, I watched the nut counter for ten or fifteen minutes without once seeing a customer steal a peanut, which is a sad commentary on the tensions in this particular community.

"Well, it was snowing the other day and I dropped in to warm my ears and confirm my observation that women in upper middle-class supermarkets never compare prices before buying canned soda pop. It was very dull—women all immaculately made up under their hair curlers, men wearing the hooded expressions of people expecting F.B.I. surveillance.

"Then I noticed this curious phenomenon. The store was full of men wearing black Russian fur hats. I say 'full of men.' Actually, there were seven Russian-hatted men out of about fifteen male customers.

"The faces of these seven were fascinating. They were all

unmistakably upper middle-class American faces, but the Russian fur hats had them under terrible strain. A Russian fur hat, I suddenly discovered, cannot be worn without making its wearer feel morose, conspiratorial, sinister, or—in a word—Russian.

"Here were these seven open, innocent American faces struggling to adapt to the personality of the hat. One fellow, clearly the son of the Chinese restaurant owner across the street, was struggling to suggest that he was a C.I.A. agent just back from a mission inside Mongolia. Another, pretty obviously a Government accountant, was buying a broom and trying to put on a cunning State Department face corrupted by too much patriotic lying and too many false compliments.

"A third, whom I recognized as a local laundry owner, was browsing in canned vegetables and struggling with the illusion that he was an evil singing master with a half-dozen *Trilbys* in his power. Another, who must have been a trigonometry teacher, labored over a huge pipe trying to look like a chap who knew more than he would care to admit about the opium route down to Singapore.

"It was tragic. All seven faces were in the power of their Russian hats and totally out of character. Their wives and mothers—these were obviously Christmas Russian hats—had wanted to make their men more mysterious, and instead had turned them into parodies.

"It struck me then that the failure of the American hat industry is having repercussions transcending the economic losses of the hatmakers. This is a country that needs a man's hat true to the American character, and the hat industry has failed to produce it. For years, because of the hat industry's lack of creativity, the American man has been forced to go around in other countries' hats.

"He may wear a bowler and be a comic Englishman, a homburg and be a comic continental, a Borsalino and be a comic Italian, an Astrakhan and be a comic Russian, or a beret and be a comic Frenchman, but the hatters offer nothing to make him a dashing American.

137

"He can wear a domestic porkpie and look like a book-maker, or a snapbrim and look like a plainclothes man, but between these extremes of caste he has no dignified option but to go bareheaded. There is nothing wrong with a bare-headed population, of course, except that it catches a lot of colds and lacks identity in a crowd.

"We ought not, however, to impose other countries' hats on it. These only make it behave foolishly at the super-market."

Squandering the kicks

Recent news from Harvard and the New York City school system ought to make American youth ask whether it is going about life in the right way.

The New York Board of Education reports a big increase in the rate at which pupils are assaulting school teachers. Between 1964 and 1965, pupil assaults had averaged one per school day, a jump of about 400 per cent over the previous year.

At Harvard marijuana consumption is said to be getting out of hand. Students there recently told a reporter, probably with extravagant boasting, that 20 to 50 per cent of the twelve thousand five hundred persons at the university will probably have tried marijuana before leaving Harvard Square.

There is something seriously wrong here, and it doesn't require a foundation study to define it. American youth is using up life too fast.

Most contemporary parents have had a taste of the prob-lem in one form or another. Who has not had to contend with the eight-year-old who insists on going to the school dance, often in the family car?

Sensible parents refuse permission. These parents realize

that dancing is a form of amusement which palls rapidly. After five or six years of dancing, most people want to move on to something new. A child who starts his dancing phase at eight will probably want to move on to gin by fourteen.

The same principle holds true for assaulting teachers and trying marijuana. The average youth of ninth or tenth grade age is too young to assault teachers.

Pupils who assault teachers at thirteen are unable to get relief from assaulting anyone less than a policeman by the time they reach twenty. More often, they simply become jaded with the whole education battle and, by the age of thirty, have no zest left for browbeating the teachers with the P.T.A.

College is too early to try marijuana. In a properly paced life, marijuana should be saved until well on into adulthood when gin has stopped working. Even then, many adults never take it on. After marijuana, they reason, the only thing left to move on to will be heroin. And heroin, they know, is the end of the line, the last kick.

What the present crop of teacher-assailants and marijuana testers fail to realize is that the kicks-content of the typical seventy-year lifetime is not very high. If they exhaust it before they get out of Harvard, they will wind up at twenty-five like those poor devils of the jet set who flit around the Mediterranean wearing purple eye pouches.

It is useless to warn young people about the dangers of using up life in their youth. They merely retort that you do not know how terrible it is to be young at a time like this.

They have a point. It was surely better to be young a generation ago when parents wouldn't let you go dancing at the age of eight, when the janitor clubbed you with a coal shovel for beating the teacher and when college presidents turned you over for infantry fodder in Germany if you fooled around with marijuana.

It was clearly understood in that generation that some of life's pleasures had to be kept in the bank to help a youth through adulthood. As a result, this country still has a large population of people who can still dance, though antiquat-

139

edly, at thirty, who can still obtain satisfactory relief from gin at forty, and who at forty-five still look forward to the pleasure of socking their first school teacher.

Modern youth's urge to burn up its limited kicks supply is understandable. Like youth since Cain's day, it comforts itself in the romantically melancholy delusion that tomorrow may never come. Alas, it always does.

We cannot expect to persuade youth of this. We can only try to persuade it by example, or tyranny if necessary, to save a little something for the bad days ahead. In normal cases it may work to call youth in during the cocktail hour and say, "Look, here I am at thirty-seven, still alive despite fifteen years of marriage to the same woman, four children to nag me night and day, a second mortgage, a used car and a job feeding index cards to a machine, and I can still carry on without going to marijuana like those creeps at Harvard."

In bad cases youth may reply, "Give me one of those martinis or I'll need a psychiatrist." Then, for youth's own good, the only humane response is to whack it across the shoulder blades with a coal shovel.

VIII

At Bay in the Twentieth Century

Right man, wrong century

The history makers have lost no time in acclaiming Sir Winston Churchill "The Man of the Century." For those of us who are as yet only in the summer of life, it is disheartening to see the award passed out at a time when the century still has nearly thirty-five years to run.

It also shows a poor grasp of history's weakness for whim. By the year 2000, when the performance records will all be complete, history is very likely to have thrown away its old 1965 measure and established new standards for judging greatness.

This, at least, is the hope that will have to sustain us middle-aged, middle-class heroes of many a well-driven traffic jam during the thirty-five years ahead. We are only too painfully aware that valor on the order of Churchill's is no longer possible for us.

It is not that we would not, if a man still could, charge with the cavalry at Omdurman, sweep the seas for England or die with Gordon at Khartoum. In our daydreams we do these things all the time, but we know with the futile bitterness of *Miniver Cheevy* that heroism of this sort is simply not Twentieth Century.

Perhaps by the year 2000 this fact will be self-evident to the people who choose the Man of the Century. Perhaps they will finally concede that while Sir Winston was an extraordinary man indeed, he was at bottom a man of the nineteenth century and that the man of the twentieth must be quite a different case.

At a guess, he will not be a warrior hero like Churchill, but a man who saw clearly that heroism had become impractical and war a transaction between machines. He will never have sat a horse, but the biographers will tell many an anecdote about his fearlessness on the expressway.

An orator? Quite possibly, but he will be remembered not for the grandeur of his rhetoric but for his sagacity in choosing ghost writers. His name may appear on a variety of books written by rented authors.

If a statesman, he will be venerated for leading his people to noble heights of goods consumption and for cheering them on to daring feats of credit purchase. In his exhortations for the people to rise up and absorb the terrible onrush of creature comforts he will urge them to "buy them on the beaches, buy them in the streets, buy them in the suburbs, buy them at the drive-in and buy them on the fourth-class mail-order postal card."

He will not be, like Churchill, a school drop-out. He will have at least seven years of college and will know more about one specific thing of absolutely no interest to anyone than any other man who has ever lived. His university will boast that its incomparable competitive pressure gave him his first ulcer.

Unlike Churchill, he will neither smoke nor drink nor otherwise live high. Steeped in the daily medical warnings of his age that living will kill you, he will be an abstemious eater of salads and yogurt. In old age, heavy with memories, he will doze by the fire and dream not of cavalry charges at Omdurman but of old half-forgotten diets, and wake grumpily to call for celery water.

Surely his days of greatness will not begin, as Churchill's did, at sixty-five. By that time he will have been forced to take a pension and move to Florida. He may possibly take up painting there, but shuffleboard is more likely.

By the year 2000, of course, his career is very likely to be closed out forcibly at the age of fifty by his company, its insurance agent or the Government. In all likelihood, he will have been celebrated as a brilliant young man to the age of thirty-nine years three hundred and sixty-four days and dismissed as an old man at forty.

From all this, two things are obvious: First, that millions of us may still qualify for "Man of the Twentieth Century"; and second, that the world lost an awfully good century when Queen Victoria died.

The stop explosion

One of the graver problems confronting this country today is the traffic-sign explosion.

"No Parking at Any Time" reproduction has exceeded the birth rate for a decade, and some demographers believe that "No Left Turn" already outnumbers homo sapiens. The appalling fertility of "Stop" and "One Way" is well known.

Lately, however, matters have become even more disturbing. A new generation of traffic signs is taking over the nation's curbstones and lamp posts with dozens of advisories and warnings which vary from the baffling to the neurotic to the arrogant.

What is interesting is the amazing ease with which the typical American brain is able to absorb all this complicated information, store it in memory cells, and produce it instantaneously for usage while directing a large, cumbersome piece of machinery through complex traffic maneuvers.

The exercises performed by the motoring brain during a typical five-mile urban drive might well make an electronic computer blush. To demonstrate, a human brain was retained and instructed to direct a car from Chevy Chase, Maryland, to the American Forestry Association in downtown Washington at 919 17th Street, a distance of 6 miles.

The memory lobes, of course, were filled with traffic sign information gathered in past Washington city driving experience. Fresh information fed into the brain included the address, the weather condition, the time, estimated time of arrival at destination, and the day of the week. Here is a record of the trip.

At Connecticut Avenue and Jocelyn Street, brain referred to time (3:57 P.M.) and calendar information (Friday), and noted that in three minutes it would have to confine car's southward movement to two of boulevard's six lanes. ("Four

145

Southbound Traffic Lanes, 7-9:30 A.M.; Two Southbound Lanes, 4-6:30 P.M., Monday Thru Friday.")

On the periphery of downtown, the brain dealt instantly with two optional route choices presented: to remain on Connecticut or veer eastward and approach destination via 18th Street. In a ten-millionth of a second or so, the memory lobes advised that at this time of this day southward movement would be forbidden on 18th Street. ("One Way North, 4-6:30 P.M., Monday Thru Friday.")

While the operator cursed traffic, the brain began transmitting downtown entry directions. With a 4:28 P.M. estimated arrival time at Rhode Island Avenue, a left turn onto 17th Street would be impossible. ("No Left Turn, 4-6:30 P.M., Monday Thru Friday.")

Consulting sign memory lobes at a furious rate, brain began long series of option rejections. Warned against left turn at I Street, noting that from I Street access to destination would be barred by "Do Not Enter" and "No Left Turn."

Rejected left turn onto 17th from DeSales Street, recalling "No Parking" signs from memory tubes. On right side of street in destination block, "No Parking 4-6:30 P.M., Monday Thru Friday." "Cars Towed Away."

Parking equally impossible on left side in front of destination. ("No Parking Entrance.") ("No Parking 7-9:30 A.M., 4-6:30 P.M. Monday Thru Friday.") ("No Parking 9:30 A.M.-4 P.M., Entrance, Monday Thru Friday.") ("No Parking 6:30 P.M. to 12 Midnight, Taxicab Stand, Two Vehicles.")

Brain, whirring furiously, began rejecting options by the dozen, lighting red warning lights in operator's self-control panel. Parking on commercial parking lot impossible, brain lobes warned. ("Sorry, Temporarily Filled" signs permanently posted.)

With incredible speed, brain almost instantly rejected all options and messaged operator that his only choices were to return to Chevy Chase, park car and take cab to destination, or proceed to Baltimore via Expressway. ("Baltimore Ex-

146

pressway Straight Ahead. Use Harbor Tunnel to New York.")

The moral is that no man with a brain should take a car downtown until something is done about these signs.

The cosmonauts' whiskers

When the Russian cosmonauts Nikolayev and Popovich made the first overnight orbit around the earth and returned from space, they needed a shave. It was too bad. These 5 o'clock shadows from the Buck Rogers future proved conclusively, for those who still had hopes, that something cosmic out there is grinning at us.

When two men strike out for that wonderful universe next door, it is depressing to know that they are going to arrive with the same old burdens of trouble and sorrow they carried back here. And that is clearly the message of the cosmonauts' beards.

After all, if a man can't even expect to leave the shaving miseries back on earth, what likelihood is there that anything else is going to be better once he gets to the other worlds?

All the evidence of both Soviet and American space travel to date indicates that instead of solving anything, travel around the cosmos is only going to make the routine problems of coping with life harder than ever. John Glenn's experiment with eating in space showed that cookies out there crumble just as cookies crumble down here. Down here they at least settle into sofa chinks and bedclothes. Out there, without gravity, they float suspended in space, where they can drift under eyelids and into delicate machinery. Add to the paraphernalia required for future space ships: a cookie-crumb net.

Schoolboys everywhere will think twice about space careers since the Russians have shown that space travel is no

147

excuse for ignoring their homework. Colonel Popovich reported that he was studying his English after his 500,000th mile and planned to get on with his physics after dinner.

Again these are difficult earth burdens made harder. Physics and English are hard enough to master under the most comfortable campus conditions. Imagine trying to come to grips with the dangling participle and adiabatic expansion while encumbered with a pressurized suit, gloves and glass helmet. And while watching a telephone that might ring any minute with a personal call from Leonid Brezhnev or Lyndon B. Johnson.

A Congressional committee has recently held hearings on the feasibility of giving the ladies a role in the American astronaut program. It takes little imagination to guess the problems this will raise when the day comes, as it surely will. Powder blending with the cookie crumbs suspended in mid-capsule, bobby pins floating into the yaw stabilizer, gloves lost on remote planets.

Add to the paraphernalia required for future space ships: an interplanetary ladies' glove-finder.

The technologists can probably supply the gadgets needed to whip all these problems. If they can shave sandpaper on television, they can shave an astronaut in weightless space without scattering whiskers all through the cookie crumbs.

They can probably devise ways to clear the cabin air of crumbs, bobby pins, face powder and even man-woman tensions. On the grander level they can probably think up ways to transport all the commonplaces of earth life, from politics to war to traffic congestion, all over the solar system.

What they cannot do, however, is build man an escape hatch to that wonderful universe next door. As the cosmonauts' beards have shown, they can only help man lug his troubles along on the search.

No one can disparage the instinct behind the search. It would be too bad, however, if it ended by blotting out the Milky Way with a curtain of celestial debris composed of old whiskers, bobby pins and face powder dumped from spaceship garbage ejectors.

Snow and the city

An urbanite's guide to snow:

I. Philosophy of Snow—One snow in a winter is happiness. Two snows are too many. Three snows are a penance visited upon cities that are unjust. Wise is the man who goes to Yucatan after the first snow, for he shall escape the ravages of dipsomania, self-pity and misanthropy, and his shoes shall not be ruined.

II. The Ideal Snow—The ideal snow starts on Saturday night, falls until Sunday afternoon to a depth of no more than four inches and, followed by a warm southerly air, melts by Monday morning.

III. Snow Crime—It is the mark of an evil nature to compel small boys to shovel snow when they desire to go sledding. Cars unable to negotiate main streets without snow tires or chains are guilty in most cities of crimes against traffic. Owners of these cars may be jailed on charges of contributing to the delinquency of traction.

IV. Snow Cream—To make this charming old American confection, hang a large pan outside the window to catch the snow. Cover the pan with cheesecloth filter to sift out soot and incinerator fallout. When the pan is filled, test with a Geiger counter for radioactivity. Boil the snow, then allow contents of pan to cool before splashing lightly on walls of freezer compartment. Set for two days, then scrape frost from freezer walls and blend with ingredients to taste, calling children to announce, "We're going to make snow cream!"

V. Snow Things to Do—Build a blaze in the fireplace. Call everyone who may be expecting an evening of your life and tell them you are hopelessly snowbound. Turn off the radio and television to shut out snow-tire salesmen and depressing weather forecast. Send the children sledding. Close the curtains. Listen to the silence.

VI. Snow Don'ts—Do not shovel the snow. Do not take

149

the sled and try to show the children how it should be done. Do not mistreat the children when you find your new homburg on the snow man.

VII. Old Snow Sayings—"Doesn't the city look lovely when it first snows?" "Let's have another drink." "My feet are wet." "You'd think Smith would at least have the decency to have his sidewalk shoveled." "Of course there'll be school tomorrow!"

VIII. Curious Facts of Snow History—It doesn't snow like it used to thirty years ago. Thirty years ago it didn't snow like it used to thirty years before that.

IX. Snow Compulsion—A phenomenon of urban snow is its power to make men behave insensibly.

For example, the first deed of seven out of ten men when a snowstorm abates is to clear the car. In the same pattern, snow-plow operators gravitate instinctively toward a freshly cleared car out of an obsessive need to rebury it while the owner is inside boasting to his wife.

Instead of giving up, the owner will feel compelled to clear it again. Then, just as helpless to resist snow compulsion, he will set out to drive a few blocks, "just to see how bad the streets are."

If the streets are sufficiently filthy with slush, he will have to accelerate as he passes pedestrians and give them splashing notice that he is the sort of fellow who can get his car cleared when others are defeated and footbound.

X. Building Snow Morale—If condemned to the city through a three-snow winter, make it an adventure. A man may imagine himself Washington waiting patiently at Valley Forge, or Marshal Kutuzov cunningly suffering the insolence of Napoleonic slush-splashers until the time is ripe to hound them out of Moscow.

Over her coffee, a woman may fancy herself on a cruise to Beirut. A man approaches her deck chair, bows and sits. He is Marcello Mastroianni. . . .

God goes mobile

It was inevitable that religion would have to yield sooner or later to the national passion for life on the run. The old form of worship involved too much lost motion for a people accustomed to living in a perpetual state of transportation. The first breaks with the old tradition of worship without an earthly destination have occurred in New Jersey. There, the Erie-Lackawanna Railroad has agreed to reserve a car on one of its morning commuter trains for regular traveling church services.

In addition, the Neshanic Reformed Church of Hillsborough, N. J., has opened a drive-in Park-and-Pray area. There is space outside the church for six cars and there are car-side racks containing sound speakers, heaters, hymn books and church bulletins.

The way American life is trending, neither park-and-pray nor the commuter church car seems like a startling innovation, but they illustrate something strange. This is a country where millions of people are supposed to have a leisure-time problem, and yet they apparently can't be separated from their wheels long enough to contemplate their place in eternity.

The explanation surely cannot be that people lack the time to sit in a church that isn't going anywhere.

The more probable explanation is rather disturbing. This, very simply, is that we may all be moving toward a state of psychological conditioning in which life becomes an endless transportation process.

We already have drive-in eating, drive-in banking and drive-in hotel registration to condition us for drive-in worship.

We court in cars at speeds up to seventy miles an hour. Is it far-fetched to expect that, before the decade is out, a couple who have discovered love on the expressway will get a

151

marriage certificate at a drive-in city hall, then speed off to the railroad station to be married in the church car? The wedding reception will be held in the bar car, of course, and then the newlyweds will go to the movies on a plane to Miami where they will pick up the house trailer for their honeymoon tour of the Interstate Highway System and be transported happily ever after.

What started the country down this road was the sensible American demand for more convenient living. The drive-in hamburger stand was a civilized and rational development. It made it quicker to eat a meal that you probably didn't want to eat anyhow, and you didn't have to look at the people who were cooking it.

With drive-in banking, the argument for convenience was a little less persuasive. It eliminated opportunity for taking a bit of healthy exercise and it did away with the excuse for looking the bank staff in the eye at regular intervals to gauge the bank's soundness.

At about this stage of things, the transportation urge was beginning to override the sensible desire for convenient living. After that, we moved into a phase where transportation became intolerable unless we were using the travel time for something besides travel. Thus began the era of the airborne theater.

From there, it has been a short step to the stage where living seems like lost motion unless carried out while moving toward a destination. In this phase, people attending a church service that is not taking them to Penn Station will feel that they are managing their lives ineffectively.

The logical conclusion to this trend is perpetual transportation. If life reaches this pass, destinations will disappear and we will live in constant transport from gas pump to gas pump.

Absurd? Not for a nation on the go. When skeptics ask where it is going so efficiently, the answer will finally be clear: To the gas pump.

The tattle-tale eyeball

Two ugly breakthroughs in the psychological science have occurred recently. One is the discovery that the pupil of the human eye expands when looking at something the beholder likes. The second is the discovery that future criminals can be detected with reasonable accuracy when they are still mere toddlers.

Knowledge of this sort can do people nothing but harm. Dr. Eckhard H. Hess of the University of Chicago, who discovered that the eye betrays its master's likes and dislikes, has already suggested an unpleasant application. Eye examinations may replace lie-detector tests.

"It is as if we are looking into the subject's brain and measuring his subjective feelings without the need of a verbal report," he said. Has it occurred to Dr. Hess that most people do not like being reduced to "subjects" and do not want their brains looked into?

In his research Dr. Hess showed a group of subjects some photographs of politicians while taking movies of their eyeballs. Some pupils dilated at Senator Goldwater, some at President Johnson, thus indicating which subjects favored which candidate.

The implications for the polling business are revolutionary. Until now the voter confronted by a polltaker could lie at will. Now, however, man's option of keeping his opinion to himself is threatened. The polltaker merely shows him a picture and photographs his eyeballs.

This is like putting a wiretap on a man's soul, and when the optics industry produces the inevitable tiny eyeball movie camera—it will be hidden in a man's tie clasp or a woman's brooch—the mischief will be endless.

"Last night you said you loved me," women will say, producing the developed film. "The pictures show you lied." Guests who have hated the dinner will no longer tell the hostess that the evening was marvelous: they will know that

153

concealed cameras may prove them hypocrites.

The paradox of the tattle-tale-eyeball discovery is that it expands knowledge but sets back civilization. Civilization is being able to tell a woman that you love her even when your back is killing you and you'd rather watch the baseball game.

Civilization is telling your hostess her party was wonderful even when she has kept you tied up all evening with the worst Gorgon in town. Civilization is being able to smile at the worst Gorgon in town without fear of having your pupils photographed. Civilization is telling the polltaker anything that will get rid of him without an ugly scene. Civilization is not having your brain looked into by busybodies.

The ability to spot a criminal while he is still in diapers is another blow to progress. Now that we have this knowledge the next step will be preventive police work. At the age of seven or thereabout the child marked for a life of crime will be taken under wing by understanding social workers who will try to interest him in constructive activities, probably skills that can be used in prison.

His parents will be told that he is a lively criminal prospect, and that they must not make any of the parental mistakes that commonly drive youth into the underworld. At school the child will be placed in the criminal's track. Emphasis will be placed upon happy social adjustment and illustrated lectures on capital punishment. The outcome is predictable to everyone who has seen the working of the track system in schools. The child assigned to the oafs' class senses immediately that he has been written off as a loser, and resigns himself to a second-rate future.

When the criminal track is added, the child assigned to the crooks' class will sense that he has been earmarked for prison and resigns himself to a life of crime. Left alone, he might enjoy twenty or thirty years of happy youth before cracking his first safe. Impressed at infancy with his criminality, he is unlikely ever to have a happy moment and very likely to start snatching jelly beans by third grade.

The trouble with psychology is that it doesn't care that reducing people to subjects is bad for people.

The hole delusion

Every American city these days has a large supply of holes. The purpose of these holes, according to the people responsible for them, is to solve problems. During the night, workers from the Municipal Holes Department fan out through the city, placing holes at heavily trafficked intersections and in the middle of important streets. Naturally, the holes cause a great deal of inconvenience. They block traffic and attract men with air hammers and steam shovels which make shattering noises.

The strange fact is that very few citizens ever question the necessity for the holes. Indeed, the national faith in the efficacy of holes seems unbounded. People assume that the hole represents America tackling a problem—providing more electric power, improved sewers, better paving, and so forth —and they adhere to the innocent notion that when the hole is removed, life will be better.

In point of fact, what actually happens when the hole is removed? Is it carted out to sea and dumped with the radioactive waste? It is not. It is simply moved to another intersection.

We tolerate the nuisance of the holes out of a dreamy faith that they will eventually make it possible for us to live in a finished world where holes will no longer be needed, although all the evidence clearly demonstrates that each problem solved by a hole creates another problem demanding another hole. In the matter of holes, America is on a treadmill.

What is touching about this, is the American faith that progress can be made by solving problems. The cruel law of life is that a solved problem creates two new problems, and the best prescription for happy living is not to solve any more problems than you have to.

The trouble with New York today is that it has been afflicted with problem-solving zealots for generations. The result is the most hole-ridden city on earth. If the zealots had

155

been content to let more of New York's problems rest unsolved, several million people would long since have decided to take up abode elsewhere and it would be possible to travel crosstown today faster than in Peter Stuyvesant's time. That would have been progress.

Instead, people like Robert Moses and Consolidated Edison dedicated their lives to solving New York's problems, with the result that New York now has more unsoluble problems than the State Department.

The time to solve a problem is when it is threatening to turn into a disaster, as the civil rights problem is now doing. The new Negro problems that are going to result from solving the civil rights problem will be plentiful and troublesome, but that risk will have to be taken.

Unfortunately, American society is so problem-oriented that it is difficult to avoid slipping mindlessly into the problem-solving state of mind. A typical pitfall is a quotation from Nat Hentoff which appeared in The New Republic.

Writing of the anarchic attitude of youth nowadays, Mr. Hentoff says that the young are protesting, among other things, "the hollowness of their parents." Nine out of ten parents who read this line, unless they are careful, are going to say, "I have a parent problem," and start devising solutions to their hollowness.

These parents will be headed for trouble. Before they realize it, they will be picketing and saying things like "existentialism" and boring people to death with earnest discussions about American morality. This is the way to dig a life full of holes. What's more, while it may solve one problem (the hollow-parent problem), it is almost certain to create several new ones.

First off, the children are bound to be embarrassed by watching a patently hollow parent try to pretend that he cares about Jean-Paul Sartre. This can only lead to a square-parent problem.

Then, the parents are going to find that earnest discussion of American morality is no substitute for lying on the sand in Miami Beach feeling that they've earned the right to hollowness. This can lead to a marriage problem. The sensible course for the typically hollow parent is to remind himself that his own parents seemed pretty hollow too, to make reservations for Miami and to tell his wife, "Ah well, the children have to be weaned sometime. There's no point in digging holes about it."

Illiac II

Does anyone really know what's going on among the new generation of machines? It is highly doubtful, although the cyberneticists who live with them keep insisting that they are really mindless brutes incapable of organizing a political takeover.

These assurances have been offered regularly for the past twenty years, while the machines have become increasingly clever. They have taken over large chunks of American industry. They have seized jobs from millions of American workers.

They have taken virtually absolute control of the nation's telephone system and do a large part of the nation's financial billing, banking and accounting. At the Pentagon they regulate American defense planning.

Nothing to worry about, the cyberneticists keep saying. It is reminiscent of the politicians of the 1930's who insisted that Hitler was really a harmless chap who liked children. The confidence of the machine-keepers would be touching if it were less sinister.

In Urbana, Ill., for example, a machine recently performed one of those grotesque mathematical problems that they are all so fond of. It proved the biggest prime number ever.

A prime number is a number that is divisible only by itself. Everyone can reel off a few small prime numbers—3, 7, 13,

157

23, etc.—but Illiac II, the machine at Urbana, was after the big ones.

The number it produced contained 2,917 digits. According to a dispatch from Science Service, proof that the number could be divided evenly only by itself took the computer 85 minutes. In this time it performed 750,000,000 multiplications and additions, a task that would have required 80,000 man years.

Moreover, before proving the new number, the machine examined 400 other numbers and did the equivalent of 8,000,000 man years of calculations.

There is an immediate economic consideration, frivolous, perhaps, but illustrative of the machines' ultimate capacity for economic mischief-making. Simple calculations that can be performed in three man minutes indicate that the 8,080,-000 man years of work performed by Illiac II would have provided lifetime employment for nearly 180,000 men.

No one is worrying about unemployment in the prime-number sector of the work force, but the point is that no one has figured out how to cope with machine-caused unemployment among either unskilled mathematicians or unskilled factory workers.

What's more, a sinister question is raised by Illiac II's achievement. How does anyone know that its 2,917 digit number is really a prime number? Will the machine's work be cross-checked by human arithmetic? Not likely.

The cyberneticists will assure us that the machine checks itself. They have faith in the machine. To them, it is inconceivable that the machine might cheat, that the machine might find it amusing to play a joke. Or that the machine might, under orders from the great machine who is masterminding the conquest of man, deliberately churn out a bogus prime number.

The evidences of a developing intellect in the machine community are scanty, but disturbing. A mischievous machine cuts an Atlanta businessman into a startling conversation between two football coaches. A meddlesome machine switches a telephoning clergyman into a conversation between divorcing man and wife, thus rescuing the marriage. The cyberneticists are laughing. They know the machines cannot think. They know that the evil mastermind, the great machine, does not exist. Of course, they have little cause to worry. When *der Tag* arrives, the cyberneticists will be spared to oil the machines and replace their burnt-out tubes.

The white collar Mafia

The most dangerous organization in the United States today is the sinister conspiracy known as "The Agency."

Even J. Edgar Hoover insists that he knows nothing about it. Its directors are unknown. No one knows where it gets its orders. The amazingly efficient mechanism which enables it to pull thousands of jobs daily without ever losing an agent is a mystery to the ablest investigators.

Even the Agency's purpose is a matter of debate. Some believe it to be a master international conspiracy against sanity. Others believe it simply a routine subversive outfit dedicated to breaking the American will by spreading frustration, fury, misanthropy, excessive smoking, peptic ulcer and rapid aging.

The one undisputable fact is this: the Agency exists. Everybody, in fact, has probably been victimized by the Agency at some time without recognizing it. Consider a typical Agency operation, the bank holdup.

A person in a hurry to cash a check enters the bank and finds long lines at the teller windows. He selects the shortest line and falls in behind a gentle little gray-haired lady. The line moves rapidly. The gentle little gray-haired lady reaches the window and from a tiny paisley purse produces forty-five checks for deposit, three account books, a sheaf of U.S. Savings Bonds to be cashed, twenty-two yellow slips that have to be signed by the teller, and a ten-pound sack of mixed coins she wants counted.

The gentle little gray-haired lady is, of course, an operative of the Agency, although she would deny it—such is the discipline of the Agency's troops—even though she were threatened with the rubber hose.

Adept at the quick change, she can slip rapidly into housewife disguise and demoralize a whole shopping center. Under Agency instructions, she grabs the last jar of olives at the grocery or lurks around bakeries until someone with a ravenous appetite for cheesecake walks in, whereupon she buys the last cheesecake in the shop.

The Agency also masterminds complicated team jobs such as the elevator torture. It has its agents watch for people who board empty elevators and push the button to go to the twelfth floor. When the doors close, an Agency operative on the second floor signals the elevator to a stop, gets in and rides to the third floor. There, he gets out while two or three other Agency people get in and push the button for a stop at the fourth floor. So it goes all the way up the shaft while the victim slowly cultivates the suspicion that life is against him.

In addition, the Agency has a huge corps of operatives posing as television repair men. If you want the set fixed in time to see "Peyton Place" they wire it so that it works perfectly from the time they leave the house until the moment "Peyton Place" comes on. At that moment, the sound dies and the screen begins showing close-ups of a violent electrical storm.

This operation, known as the TV caper, often drives the victim to demolish the set spontaneously, which is the kind of reaction that seems to please the Agency.

The ingenuity of other Agency operations can be maddening. For example, when the Agency learns that you are going to a baseball game, it sends people ahead of you into the ball park to erect wide steel posts right in front of your seat.

160

It also has people who get to the theater shortly ahead of you and break your seat springs. It will then place two agents weighing three hundred pounds apiece in seats on either side of you under strict orders not to budge when you try to get in or out.

After the show starts five or six females from the Agency with seats in the row behind may arrive noisily and drag their coats across your head. If it is raining when you leave, the Agency will have hired all the cabs in town and ordered them to drive past the theater sneering at you. Other Agency workers disguised as chauffeurs will roar past in limousines to splash you with gutter juices.

The worst part of it is that the police are simply uninterested in complaints. "The Agency?" they will ask, if you demand action at the police station. "The Agency is like the System. There's no such thing, and you can't beat it."

The police, of course, all work for the Agency.

Ben was swell, but he's out

Old saws are wearing out. Take the case of "The devil finds work for idle hands to do." As recently as fifteen years ago when a mother caught a son loafing around the pornography rack at the corner drugstore, she could take him by the ear and lead him home to wash the windows, with the perfectly satisfactory explanation that "The devil finds work for idle hands to do."

Nowadays, the world is different. With the march of automation, idleness is becoming the national occupation and sociologists will speak sternly to mothers who oppose it. Since ever-expanding idleness is the goal of the American economy, it is unpatriotic to mention it in the same breath with Beelzebub.

The goal now is to rehabilitate idleness, and the first step

161

in every rehabilitation program is a name change. During World War I, when Germany became the enemy, the Hunnish sauerkraut was restored to respectability by being renamed "liberty cabbage." In the same way, ugly satanic old idleness is now rechristened "leisure."

Leisure sounds ever so much more decent than idleness. It sounds like something that the uptown set might go in for enthusiastically. Idleness was an evil to be fought by placing such weapons as window-washing rags and lawnmowers in the hands of the indolent young. Leisure is merely another typical American problem to be solved by a nexus of committees, study groups and Congressional investigations.

Now, if a boy loafs around the pornography rack, it is merely because he has a "leisure-time problem." The solution is not to put him to work—the machines have most of the jobs well in hand—but to encourage him to take up the oboe or start a bee colony. In this way, we say, he uses his leisure "creatively."

The notion of creative leisure is mostly nonsense, of course. The sin that a boy may stumble into by keeping company with oboe players or going to bee-keepers' conventions is considerable, especially if his interest in oboes or bees is only a substitute for loafing around the drugstore.

The American economic system must, nevertheless, be justified. And so, if a boy follows the oboe path to sin, his parents are no longer permitted to blame it all on Satan; instead, the parents are indicted for failing to find a creative solution to the leisure-time problem.

There are many other pieces of ancient wisdom that have turned obsolete under the bizarre new American prosperity. Take "A penny saved is a penny earned." Sound enough in Franklin's day perhaps, but clearly subversive in 1965.

The first economic duty of every citizen today is to consume. To keep the economy booming we must consume with our cash, consume with our credit cards, consume with our charge accounts and then go to the bank to borrow the means to consume again.

It is obvious that if people began acting on the theory that

162

"A penny saved is a penny earned," production would fall, unemployment would rise, salaries would be cut and the country would stagnate. Nowadays, the homily should read, "A penny spent is not good enough."

Then there is the collapse of "A stitch in time saves nine." To maintain even the present unsatisfactory level of employment, it is absolutely imperative that we never settle for the timely one-stitch job when a bit of dallying can make work for nine additional stitchers.

As we have seen in too many industries, the nine stitchers thrown out of work either go on relief—which reduces the timely stitcher's take-home pay—or turn in desperation to braining the smug stitch-in-time takers for their entire pay envelopes. In this type of economy, the canny stitcher takes his stitch too late.

And, of course, there is old "Early to bed and early to rise makes a man healthy, wealthy and wise." Taken literally, this advice would now be disastrous.

In the first place, rising early would immediately raise the leisure-time problem to unmanageable proportions. The safest of all leisure-time activities is sleep, and the fellow who rolls out at cock's crow to work on his oboe is going to be thoroughly sated with leisure by breakfast time.

What's more, early rising tends to make a man reflect on the absurdity of his life. In this mood, he may very well realize that his way of life is insane and decide to change it by saving a penny, thereby triggering an economic catastrophe.

Very likely he will go to the office feeling energetic and healthy and, before he can stop himself, take a stitch in time, thus causing unemployment, raising his taxes and increasing crime. "Early to bed and early to rise" has had its day.

So, apparently, has Benjamin Franklin.

The spreading decline

"And when did you first notice this numbness?" asked the doctor.

"In a cab. It was Friday. The driver had the radio on and the news came on and somebody said that the Chinese Communists had just exploded a nuclear bomb. To my horror I noticed that I was taking the news with perfect equanimity."

"What did you say to the cab driver?"

"I looked out at the trees, which were turning gold and red, and I said, 'My, the trees are coming on right pretty now, aren't they?' "

"You were utterly incapable of crying 'Wow!' or 'My God!' despite the horrifying news that the Chicoms at last had the bomb?"

"I couldn't even work up an 'Oh boy!' "

"Hm."

"Exactly. I thought to myself, 'Hm. I'm going numb.' I tried to worry about it. I went to the office and leafed through newspapers, hoping to revive my capacity for outrage. Britain had just elected a galloping Socialist. The Communists had just thrown out Khrushchev. The Yankees had just blown the World Series. All I could feel was a gentle yearning to drive to the mountains and look at the foliage."

The doctor stifled a yawn. "Although there were titanic struggles going on all around you," he said, "you were unable to make yourself care."

"Titanic struggles suddenly meant nothing to me, Doctor. Suddenly I realized I had spent a lifetime being horrified, fascinated, shocked, enthralled by titanic struggles whose outcome I had been powerless to influence. It was as though I had used up all my power for savoring a good titanic struggle and simply wanted the world to go away."

"Let's test those old reflexes," the doctor said, turning on a television set. A gasoline salesman appeared, followed

closely by a well-barbered young man who smiled and said,
"Worry, worry, worry! Crisis! Bomb! Scandal! Doomsday!
Titanic struggle! Soft on Communism! Struggle for men's
minds . . . !"

"What are you feeling?" asked the doctor.

"I feel an irresistible impulse to go to the refrigerator for a
beer."

The doctor produced two beers and turned off the TV.
"Has the same effect on me," he said. "Sometimes I think the
whole world has become a time-killer meant to stimulate
beer consumption."

"Then you have the numbness too?"

The doctor smiled. "Yes," he confessed. "Mine goes back
to the sixteenth or seventeenth Berlin crisis. In 1958 or
1959, I believe. Up to that time, I had been a conscientious
citizen. I spent so much time worrying about the East-West
struggle that I didn't have time for my wife and children. In
the middle of this particular Berlin crisis, I suddenly realized
that the world was completely out of my hands. It gave me
the most intense feeling of relief. I promptly tripled my fees,
joined a country club and took regular Caribbean cruises."

"What a terribly bad citizen you must be."

"I suppose so," said the doctor. "But there's nothing I can
do about it. It's not my fault I was born in the twentieth
century with a fresh titanic struggle to be absorbed at every
meal. By the age of forty these days, the average man's
alarm mechanism is shot."

"But can't you give me something to make me lie awake
worrying at night?"

"Easiest thing in the world," said the doctor. "Wait until
you get my bill. I've done more to revive my patients' capacity for outrage than all the speeches of Barry Goldwater."

VIIII

This Strange Now-ness

Who can't happen

"May I help you?" asked the Cromley & Swotts Culture Consultant.

"I want to happen," the customer said.

"Marvelous," said the C.C. "When people come in with that kind of attitude, we can do something for them. If I may say so, sir, you look as if you haven't happened for the last two or three years."

The customer said, yes, that was just what his girl had told him the night before when he had her up to his pad and offered her some fizzy gin and put on the jazz music and gave her his spiel about the literary importance of J. D. Salinger. She had said, "The trouble with you is, you're not happening." And that ended everything in the shank of the evening.

The Culture Consultant, who had heard all this many times, was ready with his soften-'em-up lecture on the cultural importance of now-ness. "The reason you're not happening," he said, "is because, culturally speaking, you're way back there in the then-ness. Pads, fizzy gin, jazz, and Salinger were then. They are simply not happening any more. They are not now. Do you understand?"

"All I understand," said the customer, "is that I want to be in on the now-ness."

"Very well," the C.C. said. "Cromley & Swotts will undertake to have you switched on." He rang and a culture technician appeared. "One non-happener to be plugged in," he said. "Calls his apartment a 'pad.' Serves fizzy gin. Listens to jazz and talks about Salinger."

"Are you sure he isn't dead?" the technician asked.

"Better start him with the injection," the C.C. said. "Straight into the brain. Full power."

169

RUSSELL BAKER

Without warning, the technician produced a transistor radio and laid it against the customer's ear. Bweem-bweem-bweem-bweem-bwoing-bwoing-bweem numberee-bwoing-twenty-bweem seven on this week's Freddie and the Dreambweemahs!"

The customer's scream faded into the shriek of electronic cataclysm tuned in through the transistor. Violent struggle. The transistor crunched under the customer's heel. "I can't stand rock 'n' roll. I've been running away from it ever since I was razor-cut in 1947 while dancing to 'Drinking Wine Spodee-Odee.' Anyhow, it's kid music."

"Not any more," the technician said. "It's what the real intellectuals listen to now and it's not rock 'n' roll. It's the sound, man! The sound. It's now! It's here! It's happening!"

"All right. I'll take two transistors," the customer said.

"Mainline it right in the ear," said the technician. "Get the *now* feel of it. Let is boing around inside the old medulla and twitch down the ganglia and you'll start to happen before you know it."

The technician went to the stockroom and came back with $75 worth of old comic books. "All these old comics—Batman, Captain Marvel, Mandrake the Magician—these are what's happening in reading," he said.

"But those are then things," the customer said.

"They're so then that they're now," the technician explained. "Come with me." He led the customer into a hideous room. "You'll need $3,000 worth of vinyl furniture and two dozen soap boxes," he said. "How about magenta or coral in the vinyl and Fab in the box line?"

"But this stuff will make my place look like a roadside burgerama," the customer protested, recoiling before a lavender vinyl escritoire.

"It's what's happening," the technician said. "Do you want people laughing at you with that old fusspot Williamsburg Restoration stuff? It went out with Tom Jefferson. Vinyl is here. It's now."

It was three hours later when the customer reappeared before the Culture Consultant to sign for his new personality. The transistor was pumping the bweem-bwoings into his

170

medulla, and he had a Brillo carton under one arm, a copy of "Dick Tracy Meets Stooge Viller" under the other, and a season pass to the Demolition Derby in his teeth.

"Can't you stop him from twitching long enough to sign the check?" the C.C. asked the technician.

"You wanted him to happen," the technician said. "I got him happening. When I cut out his medulla bwoings, he just goes numb. Look." And the technician switched off the transistor. The customer's twitch sighed to a halt and his jaw and eyes went slack. "Boy! Is he ever now!" said the C.C.

"How long do you think it'll last—this business of having to be lowbrow to be highbrow?" asked the technician.

"Not much longer," the C.C. said. "When middlebrows like this creep start getting switched on, the smart crowd will turn to something new to keep from getting lost in the mob. I'll tell you a secret, son. The smart crowd is never going to let the creeps really happen."

Which wave to the future?

Cheng Ting-chang used to sit up all night playing poker. This was before the Communist party showed him the folly of trying to draw to an inside straight. Now Cheng spends his spare time studying the works of Mao Tse-tung. "I find great happiness in it," Cheng declares in a letter to a Canton newspaper.

Cheng's confession illustrates why Americans have trouble coming to grips with China. It is inconceivable to the American mind that a young man could find great happiness in the writings of any politician, let alone one like Mao, whose prose style is thickly clotted with brain-glazers like "deviationism," "capitalistic imperialism" and "exploitation of the masses."

It is all so hopelessly old-fashioned. All those Chengs

171

sitting around reading the Gospel according to Mao in prime time. It's like Salem, Mass., in the seventeenth century or Scotland on Sunday, and because the Chinese won't let American reporters in to verify its existence, the whole place seems as unreal as a kingdom by the Grimm brothers.

Take the poker playing. The Chinese Government is worried about youth's penchant for poker. "Right after work," a newspaper complained, some young people "meet in a group for poker games, eagerly keeping at it until the small hours." Others, the paper goes on, "go window-shopping or kill their time at the teahouse; some dress or pretty up for dating and romancing until late at night."

The recommended therapy for these people is deeper immersion in the works of Mao. It's as if President Johnson decreed that American youth must quit dancing the monkey and devote their leisure to the speeches of Warren G. Harding.

The mystery is how China has been able to sell its wave-of-the-future line to the world's disgruntled. Here is this enormous country ruled by a lot of old men who are against window-shopping, poker, dating and romance and who want everybody to sit around reading political tracts.

And those rallies where everybody gets together in their quilts to sing hate songs. What do they do after those rallies? Do they go off to the teahouses to play poker or romance until late at night? Small chance. They go home and gulp down large draughts of Mao. This is a future?

If Americans are peculiarly hostile to Mao's China, it is probably due to the natural tension between age and youth. China has become uniquely an old man's country, with the old man's crotchety distaste for the frivolities of youth, while the United States has become the land of the young with youth's contempt for the *status quo*.

Youth's conquest of America can be documented in the election returns since 1960, in the story of the civil rights movement or in popular and governmental responses to the new wave of campus protest against this and that. But the best evidence is the market place, where youth's tastes now dominate.

Television, the center of American retailing, is now tailored almost exclusively for the 12-to-17 age group. Its most popular shows are a fairy tale about a witch, some cowboys tied to their father's apron strings, and a Marine Corps half-wit.

Radio, the other big marketing medium, has fallen to howlers with that long matted hair the children love because they know the grown-ups hate it. Men's clothes have acquired the stovepipe silhouette pioneered by London's juvenile gangs a decade ago, and the hottest feminine fashion from Paris is the Courrèges line which makes women look like monster 4-year-olds, all kneecaps and Rebecca of Sunnybrook Farm eyeballs.

The old people (which now means anybody over 17) are bullied by the youth czars—counterparts of Peking's old-age tyrants—into straining their lumbars in the kiddie kootch dances, drinking soda pop that makes them think young and trying to find artistic merit in comic strips. And on and on.

China and America. Age and youth. And there are all those people in between wondering which is the wave of the future. They must see quite clearly that China is not. And yet, when they look at America, which probably is, they must also ask the same question that Americans ask in dismay about China: *This* is a future?

The bacchanalia gap

Malcolm Muggeridge, the English writer, reports that "America is drenched, if not submerged, in sex." Writing in The New Statesman, he describes a country that makes Sodom and Gomorrah sound by comparison like Philadelphia on a Sunday afternoon.

Sample: Sex "permeates every corner and cranny of life, from birth to grave. Dating begins at 9 years old and even earlier; tiny tots wear padded bras, paint their faces and howl

173

like randy hyenas at the Beatles. Young lovers arm themselves with. . . ."

But let the curtain be decorously drawn, for Mr. Muggeridge's prose has scarcely begun to quiver at this point,
and what follows will have a familiar ring to conscientious
magazine readers. Scarcely a mail arrives without bringing
a magazine or two containing one of these juicy reports on
what is invariably called "The Sexual Revolution."

The message seldom varies: America is one enormous
wild party. Look, Ma! We're decadent! Wring your hands,
lick your chops and read what a wonderfully immoral bunch
we are!

It is the stock magazine piece of the 1960's. In the late
1950's they scolded us for too much cholesterol and flabby
muscles. Now it's moral rot. Does this kind of thing really
scare people?

The answer is certainly "No." What it does do is make
people feel that they are missing out on the scandalous life.
Constant exposure to these shocked reports that America
is a wild party may alarm the naive, but the sensible person
will eventually start wondering why he never receives an
invitation. Is he out of the mainstream? Is he un-American?

In his world, dating does not begin at 9 years old or earlier
and, though there is some randy hyena-like howling at the
Beatles, it is nothing more to him than a leering reminder
that parental responsibility makes it impossible to drench or
submerge himself in anything more erotic than a hot bath.

In the bath, with the Beatle-howling rising about him, he
may read these reports of the wild party that is America
and tell himself that life is passing him by. If he is over the
age of twenty-one, he knows better. He has been to too
many parties. He knows what really goes on at them. They
are all celery stuffed with cheese, women flushed with ex-
citement about the P.T.A., cigar smoke and talk of insurance policies and politicians.

He has heard all his life about the wild parties. First in
the fraternity house, then in the barracks. Men who claimed
to have attended these wild parties inflamed his imagina-

174

tion. But when he went with these very men in search of bacchanalia, it always turned out to be beer and pretzels and, later, celery stuffed with cheese.

With age, he slowly accepted the drab truth: In the average city of three million people the number of wild parties held in the average year can be counted on the fingers of one hand. What is worse, these four or five wild parties are always attended by the same people—a handful of professional wild-party goers and five hundred magazine writers who are gathering material for articles on sex-drenched America.

Every sensible adult knows that his chances of ever attending one of these parties are as remote as his chances of seeing a 9-year-old out on a date. The profound fact behind the big bull market for decadence reports is that there are millions of Americans, men and women, who know all too well that they will arrive at Social Security age without ever having experienced anything wilder than a wink from a widower or a convention night in Chicago.

These millions account for what the Muggeridges wrongly describe as "The Sexual Revolution." To fill out what they feel to be blank spots in their lives, they gobble the fantasies of the new novelists and sit through the ordeal of "La Dolce Vita" with its tantalizing view, for the decadence-starved, of what fun decadence can be.

People who are genuinely sex-drenched and bored with the orgiastic excesses are unlikely to spend their time reading such stuff and watching imitations on the screen. Such people, as we know from the newspapers, prefer golf or sitting about in bad air trying to numb their central nervous systems.

The popular success of "The Sexual Revolution" article is its own argument against the Muggeridge case. Only the moral pay good money for sermons.

Moon crisis

When, in early 1969, the time came to select the first astronaut to go to the moon, American space officials discovered that they had made a dreadful miscalculation.

The entire national supply of able-bodied nice guys had been used up in the earlier preparatory space programs such as Mercury and Gemini. "Do you mean to tell me there isn't a single nice guy left who's fit to represent America on the moon?" the President asked his space ministers.

Somebody pointed out halfheartedly that there was always Jones, who had a good clean jaw line and a winning smile. And somebody else said this was true enough, but Jones also had that bad habit of cracking jokes during press interviews instead of talking sincere.

"Nice guys don't joke about projects that are costing the voters forty billion dollars," the President decreed. "At least not while I'm running the country."

The ministers ran through the rest of the list. Brown was ruled out because he didn't televise well. Smith televised well enough, but his wife looked too voluptuous to persuade anybody that her husband could be a nice guy. Morgan and his wife both came across nice on television, but one of their children was a budding nut who pulled wings off flies.

Claiborne was out of the question. He had a Deep Southern accent, and there were already too many questions about why Dixie was getting all the space gravy. Deakin was too dark, although he cut a fine nice-guy figure. "A man that dark has got to have too many social problems to be a nice guy deep down," somebody said. "And suppose he turns out to be a secret member of the N.A.A.C.P."

Clark read poetry, which meant he might go poetic on the moon and radio back descriptions that would make the viewing audience feel illiterate. Poe didn't go to church. Evans hated cats. Skidmore liked racy women and drinking

all night. Archer's mother had once belonged to the John
Birch Society and Ellsworth was a braggart.

Once, in an interview, when asked if any finely conditioned
American of average intelligence could not pilot a capsule
to the moon, Ellsworth had said, "Of course not. This is a
job that takes extraordinary brains and guts." N.A.S.A. had
succeeded in squelching the interview, but the thought of
the crowing transmissions Ellsworth might send from the
moon was an agency nightmare.

"What about Humboldt?" the President asked. "It says
here that his nice-guy fitness rating is 98 per cent."

"What do we have on Humboldt?" the Chief Minister
asked his astronaut selection division secretary. "Humboldt,
Humboldt," the secretary murmured, as he riffled the per-
sonnel files. "Ah, here he is." And he began reading.

"Hm," he said. "Humboldt would be a natural, all right.
Telegenic. Sincere. Telegenic family. No accent. Goes to
church. Unexceptionable parents. Reading confined to jour-
nals of electronics. Good jaw line. Nondescript skin coloring."

"Humboldt makes a good speech, too," an aide said.

"Great teeth," said another. "Sound dresser, too. His
slacks aren't so wide that they're square, nor so narrow that
they're flash."

"For nice-guyness, we can't top Humboldt," the secretary
said. "He'd make everybody tuned in on the flight proud to
be American, except for one thing."

"What's that?" the President asked.

"He's chicken," said the secretary.

"Are you sure you've canvassed the entire nice-guy population?" asked the President's brother.

"There's only one other possibility," the Chief Minister
said. "I hesitate to mention him, sir, but . . ."

"Go ahead, man," the President said.

"Well, sir. It's Barry Goldwater." There was a long uneasy pause. The President and his brother conferred in whis-
pers. Finally, the President said, "In view of the fact that we
seem to have a nice-guy gap vis-à-vis the Russians, it would
be wasteful to risk a nice guy like Barry on this kind of trip."

Another pause. At length, the President leaned forward intently. "Gentlemen," he said. "There is only one man left to make this trip. When the Apollo blasts off, I shall be aboard."

"But, Mr. President!" the ministers protested. "You can't."

"You can't mean it," said the President's brother. "Say you don't mean it, Teddy. . . ."

Hard idling

Every once in a while it is important to do nothing. Whenever you find yourself dreaming of Everett Dirksen, when you catch yourself in a crowd talking like Dean Rusk, if you can't get Lyndon Johnson off your mind for weeks at a time or find that you are going to Ingmar Bergman movies when Sophia Loren is playing in the next block—then, it is time to stop everything and start doing nothing.

Nothing is harder to do. Some Puritan perversity in the American character makes us hate the nothing-doers of the world. A man quietly doing nothing is a challenge to the American system. He must be cajoled, badgered and, if necessary, blackguarded into purposeful living.

If a man inherits millions, it is thought disgraceful if he devotes them to a lifetime of doing nothing. He is expected to run for President. You see them all over the map, these wretched millionaires, wasting perfectly good fortunes on billboards, ghost writers and campaign planes and slapping backs up and down the countryside. All because of the American hatred for doing nothing.

Their wives work doughnut machines and nag people to give blood on their lunch hours. The tradition runs from top to bottom of the society. As the working stiff gets more and more leisure, he is urged to put it to hard use. On weekends, instead of dozing in a hammock, he will be found in his cellar doing cabinet carpentry, or perspiring through open fields trying to knock a ball into a hole in the ground.

The idea of using good time to do nothing offends the community. Go to a vacation spa, ostensibly devoted to the doing of nothing, and the social pressures to undertake strenuous activity are overwhelming. Tense gentlemen smelling of gymnasiums accost you over the hedge.

"What are you doing?"

"I am lying in the grass."

"Getting a sun tan, eh?"

"No. When I lay down here, the hedge was shading me, but the sun has moved now and it's too much bother to move."

"Just lying in the grass?" By this time, the inquisitor's voice will have taken on that slight edge of suspicious hostility suggestive of a Mississippi sheriff faced with a Yankee schoolboy. "What are you lying in the grass for?"

"I've been talking like Dean Rusk. I'm trying to get over it."

"I see. Vacationing. Play golf?" And the interrogation becomes uncomfortable. People who do not play golf are expected to play tennis or squash. Afternoons, they are expected to sail or churn around in motorboats. People who don't do any of these things are expected to fish. All these can be gratifying pastimes in their place, but they have nothing whatsoever to do with doing nothing.

Golf is nerve-wracking, frustrating and laborious. You have to make appointments to use the holes and go to the tailor for pastel clothes. Tennis and squash require great stamina. In sailing, you have to worry constantly where the wind is coming from, and in a motorboat you are kept busy recovering children who fall overboard. Fishing—well, it was easy when you could dangle a worm from a hickory limb, but nowadays it is a science as elaborate as biophysics.

So, there you are, lying in the grass doing nothing but feeling the ant crawl up your cowlick or, at night, counting stars in the Milky Way, and word of it spreads all over the community. People call you up and offer to lend their tennis rackets, or drop by and suggest you ought to go deep-sea fishing with them and fight the big ones.

People lying in the grass doing nothing put the whole community on edge. All that idleness—it is like having an infection in the neighborhood. People talk about it. "Doesn't do anything at all, you say?" "Says he's trying to stop talking like Dean Rusk." "Must be some kind of nut."

It doesn't seem that doing nothing used to be as hard as it is nowadays. There was a time not too long ago when it was possible to lie in the grass all summer long and let the breeze cleanse the mind of old junk and make room for big, long thoughts.

That, of course, was before everybody got rich enough to own golf clubs, boats, and memberships in squash clubs, and to sneer at a worm on a hickory pole. At that time, doing nothing was still considered antisocial, but when people sat down to do it they didn't make it hard work.

Martini failure

This all happened at lunch at The Table of the Six Borgias, and a man who was there swears it's the truth.

Four of those scrupulously barbered executive types who buy and sell actors and fly around on jets had settled into a table that counted, and Ivo, the suave Yugoslav waiter from Akron, came to take their drink orders.

"I'll have a Tanqueray martini with a slice of lemon peel," says one. "Make mine a Lamplighter on the rocks," says another. "Vodka martini, extra dry," says the third, "and make sure the vodka is Polish."

"And yours, sir?" Ivo asked the fourth man.

"I'll have a martini," he says.

"I beg your pardon," says Ivo.

"A martini."

180

"What kind of martini?" asks Ivo.

"I don't care," the fellow says. "Just a martini."

One of his companions, sensing the start of a social crisis, moved helpfully to head it off. "Bill," he says, "maybe you'd like an American vodka martini, seven-to-one, with California vermouth and an olive stuffed with anchovy."

"No," says Bill. "Really, all I want is just a martini." And, apparently feeling that the subject was closed, he turned to the fellow on his right and started talking about tax-free municipals.

Ivo's face by this time was a study in despair, but being a discreet waiter, he glided off to the bar. In a few moments he returned with the bartender. "About your martini, sir," the bartender says to Bill. "How do you feel about a Beefeater extra dry with a twist of lemon and rocks on the side?"

"Oh, I don't care," says Bill, "as long as it's a martini." And he resumed his conversation, which by this time dealt with some skyscrapers he was buying as a tax dodge. The bartender, who had been hired at great expense because he was famed for his temperament, flew off in a rage to give the *maître d'hôtel* his resignation.

Soon, the *maître d'hôtel* returned to the table with Ivo and the bartender in train and, turning his most oleaginous smile on Bill, purred, "In regard to Signor's martini . . ."

"Yes," says Bill, "I'd like to have it right now."

"If I may take the liberty to suggest, Signor, our bartender, Cesare here, makes the most exciting bourbon Americano in North America, which I am certain Signor will find far more gratifying than a martini."

"I don't want bourbon," says Bill. "I want my martini."

"With an olive?" asks the *maître d'hôtel*.

"It doesn't make any difference."

"Eight-to-one?"

"However you make them."

"Have a Limehouse yellow gin," says one of Bill's companions. "With a South African vermouth," says another. "It's what everybody's drinking on Madison Avenue this week."

181

"And have it served in a frosted Madeira glass," the third man suggests, "with a sprig of parsley."

"Or with tiny pearl onions," the *maître d'hôtel* suggests, kissing his fingertips. "The Table of the Six Borgias uses only the choicest pearl onions from Andalusia. They have been marinated for four years in Icelandic herring brine to bring out the juniper essence of Limehouse's quality gin."

It's nice of you all to plan my martini for me," Bill says, "but I think I'll just have it regular."

Ivo glared. Cesare glared. The *maître d'hôtel* glared.

The three retreated for a conference behind a Michelangelo sculpture. They telephoned the owner. "Just give him any old gin you've got around the place and a little vermouth in a cocktail glass," the owner said.

"But suppose it leaks to the press," said the *maître d'hôtel*. "We'd be the laughing stock of the overpriced restaurant racket."

"I'll be right over," said the owner. He arrived shortly afterward with a large sergeant of police. "What seems to be the trouble here?" the sergeant asks Bill. "This man insists on making a scene," says the *maître d'hôtel*.

"All I want, sergeant, is a martini," says Bill.

"Oh," says the sergeant, "one of those troublemakers. Now, are you going to leave quietly or do we run you in for creating a disturbance in a public accommodation?"

"Throw him out!" cried Bill's companions, who were now confronted with the shattering probability of never again being able to get a table that counted. "The bum probably doesn't even have a credit card," said the owner as Bill was shown the door.

"Now, sergeant," he said, "what about a little refresher?"

"Don't mind if I do," said the sergeant. "Make it a ten-to-one on the rocks, with Italian vermouth and three lime seeds in a chilled water tumbler lined with cheesecloth. And see that he stirs it exactly seven times."

IX

The Time They Ran Barry:

An Incoherent History of the 1964 Presidential Campaign

CALIFORNIA-GOTHAM: Twice nicked is not slain, sweet Petroleum. Pray tell me what letters thou hast bearing upon the mind of our irresolute Pennsylvania, dour Scranton.

PETROLEUM: Why, good my twice-nicked fellow, nature has so blended in him the qualities of mystery, silence and enigmatic countenance that no man can tell what passeth through his mind.

They say that at his whelping stars paused in their course and the dead walked unlocked from their graves foretelling deadlock that would uplift young Pennsylvania to pluck at a crown. I fear him much. Hie us now at cock's crow each our separate way ere evil eye detect us and give the game away.

CHORUS: Thus do I chorus to this history, the sundry plots expose. Ask not the ending yet, I pray, for only heaven knows.

The political junkshop

Over the door a weathered sign said "Political Supplies." It was a bad section of town, full of broken windows and doomed children, and inside the shop dank vapors curled off the walls. A spider, interrupted at his crocheting, scampered for cover and a figure compounded of charcoal-gray mist materialized in the shadows.

"You are the gentleman who wanted to see the Drain," he said. "An odd request. The first we have ever had, at least in my time."

"Well, you see—." Explanations seemed in order. "A Goldwater man told me the other night that Cuba had gone down the Drain, and I asked him where the Drain was kept. You see, for years I've heard of things going down the Drain —China, Southeast Asia, Africa."

"And," the shopkeeper interrupted, "you naturally wanted

to see if the Drain was big enough." He laughed unpleasantly. "We keep it in the cellar if you care to see it, though I must warn you that the steps are rickety and there are no lights and there is little else down there to make the trip worthwhile, unless of course, you are interested in seeing the Ratholes of the World."

"The Ratholes of the World! So you have those too."

"Oh, yes," the shopkeeper replied, "we handle the only full line of political accessories in the country, including a complete set of the Ratholes of the World. Let me show you something." He blew the dust from a glass case and lifted an ancient greenback.

"This," he said, "is one of the most famous political implements in America—the Taxpayer's Dollar."

"But I thought it had been thrown down the Ratholes of the World." The man winked, restored the greenback, and moved to another showcase.

"There was one of our biggest items twenty-five years ago," he said, pointing to a plate of shapeless, moldy nuts. "You may be too young to remember them."

"Not at all. Those are England's Chestnuts, which the politicians said we should stop pulling out of the fire."

"Ah," said the shopkeeper. "I see you are a connoisseur. Let me show you some of our finer items." He went to the rear of the shop and turned on a gray light. "You will like this," he said, indicating what appeared to be a gardening corner.

A tub of greenish water sat on the floor. "The Mainstream of the Republican party," he said. "In great demand this year."

"And here," he said, pointing to an enormous piece of asphalt covered with yellow paint, "is the Middle of the Road, sufficiently sized to accommodate any number."

"But what is that extraordinary mass of moving earth there on the table?"

"That," said the shopkeeper, "is a genuine Groundswell. Notice how the earth heaves up. We also have this remarkable Groundsurge, in which the earth heaves itself both up and forward. The candidates love to claim them, you know."

"But how do they work?"

"Quite simple. The politician needs only a set of Grass Roots, which we supply very reasonably. He then sets fire to the Grass Roots, and this activates the Groundswell mechanism."

The shopkeeper led the way upstairs, passing a corridor full of empty glass cupboards. "Gaps," he explained. "Foreign policy Gaps, defense Gaps, missile Gaps, anti-missile missile Gaps. A very big item in 1960, but a slow mover this year."

"There are two popular items," he said, indicating a garish chartreuse fringe tacked to a cupboard and an ingenious feathered creation which fluttered hopelessly inside an iron cage.

"The Radical Fringe," he said, "and the Liberal Wing." He stopped before a cell door. Inside, a ghastly shapeless mass seemed to be edging toward the light. "Creeping Socialism. An enormous seller year after year. Can I show you some Bleeding Hearts or perhaps some Extremists on Both Sides?"

"Thanks, no. I'm afraid all these relics would make it terribly hard to think clearly about the campaign."

"The whole point of our service," the shopkeeper replied. "As we tell our candidates, a voter with a mind full of junk is a voter who can't do any dangerous thinking."

Polisqueak

Candidates for the doctorate in Polisqueak are now taking oral examinations. Let's eavesdrop:

"Young man, we insist that all candidates for the doctorate must speak Polisqueak as fluently as candidates for the

189

Presidency, so if you will make a few typical Polisqueak sounds I will check your accent."

"Let us rekindle the sacred fire of liberty. I view with alarm and incredulity. No sacrifice is too great. Every American must have the opportunity. We must not flag in our historic mission . . ."

"That will do nicely. You show a gift for inanity that should carry you to the broad sunlit uplands of ghostwriting if you have the courage to leave no stone unturned. Now, what is the semantic location of conservatism?"

"Conservatism, sir, lies just to the left of the right and slightly to the right of center. To the right of the right lie, respectively, the far right, the radical right, the right-winged extremists and the lunatic fringe, in that order."

"What must we never do to the right-wing extremists?"

"We must never suppress their precious American right to dissent and never heed the reckless counsel of extremists —whether of right or left—who have lost their faith in America and seek, whether naively or through allegiance to alien ideologies, to poison the wellsprings of American life."

"Identify ten species of liberals."

"There are the Republican liberals, the Northern liberals, the so-called liberals, the phony liberals, the knee-jerk liberals, the old New Deal liberals, the Southern liberals, the agrarian liberals, the wild-eyed liberals and the liberals with quotation marks around them, who make a mockery of true liberalism."

"What curious physical characteristics do all liberals have in common?"

"They have bleeding hearts. They are not hard-nosed."

"And liberals are unsuitable to govern because . . . ?"

"They have never met a payroll. They are spenders and budget busters. They lack fiscal responsibility. They believe every problem can be solved by passing a law. They would bankrupt Uncle Sap with their crackpot schemes and dreams. They are do-gooders."

190

"Name four Republican candidates and give their identifying adjectives."

"There's Barry Goldwater, the ruggedly handsome Southwestern conservative. Harold Stassen, the perennial boy wonder. Richard Nixon, the unsuccessful 1960 G.O.P. standard bearer. And Nelson Rockefeller, the boyishly charming New York Governor whose divorce . . ."

"Very good. Extemporize on me-tooism."

"For thirty long years me-tooism has led the Republican party down the road to defeat. The great party of Lincoln must turn its back on the Eastern internationalists and the New York money crowd and refresh itself at the grass roots of the old Republican heartland."

"Very well. What do key Democrats do in Congress every election year?"

"Key Democrats huddle at the White House, plan strategy behind closed doors, confer privately with powerful Southern obstructionists and otherwise work overtime to speed up the legislative mill."

"And to what do seasoned Capitol observers always attribute the failure to speed the Congressional mill?"

"To the powerful House Rules Committee, to the influential but little-known chairman of the Senate Appropriations Committee and to the powerful Southern oligarchs cloaked in the privileges of seniority."

"What must the President do?"

"He must seek a mandate. He must sharpen his image, mend his political fences, seize the middle ground, give a strong lead, take bold new initiatives and/or departures, take to the stump, turn back the challenge, take off the gloves, stop partisanship at the water's edge, shrink before no sacrifice, leave no possible path to peace unexplored, strike back hard . . ."

"And what must the voters do?"

"The voters must plug their ears, sir, and hold onto their shirts."

191

San Francisco-I

On a typical day at the 1964 Republican Convention, these are the things that happen:

Six hundred people, give or take a dozen, will approach you and ask, "Isn't this a lovely city?" It is not enough to answer, "Yes." The approved answers are "magnificent," "breathtaking," "enchanting," or "the most charming city in America."

Five or six people will caution that you must never refer to it as "Frisco." People who call it "Frisco" betray themselves as uncultured, unworldly and, in general, the kind of people who eat soup with a coffee spoon. Besides that, it offends the natives, who have very delicate sensibilities.

Everybody, without exception, will ask where you ate last night. They will ask you to agree in principle that the restaurants here are magnificent. The approved reply is, "superb." It is all right to brag a bit about your dinner check, particularly if it exceeded $30 for two.

Between meals, you will go to observe the remnants of the Convention. These are visible chiefly in three hotels—the St. Francis, the Hilton and the Mark Hopkins, which you refer to as "The Mark," to show that you know a thing or two about soup spoons.

The Mark is the headquarters for Governor Scranton, whom you call "Bill," to demonstrate that you are on top of the political picture, and for Senator Goldwater, whom you call "Barry" for the same reason.

In the lobby of The Mark you will witness "demonstrations" which mark the coming and going of Bill and Barry. In a typical demonstration, two hundred or three hundred people, mostly in late adolescence, shout "We Want Bill!" or "We Want Barry!" depending on which one they want, and wave blue balloons. Older people will shout at you, asking "Isn't this a lovely city?" or "Where did you eat last night?"

The St. Francis is for viewing demonstrators and the Platform Committee. The demonstrators carry signs bearing such messages as: "Earl Warren and the Supreme Court justices who are against God, the Bible, our nation and for Communism had better repent now."

The Platform Committee sits inside in an overheated room, listening to the dullest speeches conceivable. Later they will produce a paper, which Bill's people will denounce and nobody will read.

At the Hilton Hotel, you will see the press, small-bore politicians, candidates and candidates' aides as they perform for television. Bill's people will press you into corners and say things like, "It's terrible," and "What's going to happen to the two-party system?" and "Isn't this a lovely city?"

Barry's people will be strolling about trying to look reasonable and not too smug. If approached, they will take you aside and enumerate the subjects on which Barry has been misquoted and tell you what they paid for dinner last night.

Occasionally, Barry himself may be seen. For anyone expecting the lordliest conservative since the Duke of Wellington, he will be a disappointment. His wardrobe of political clichés is impeccable but undistinguished.

In a typical display before the Platform Committee, for example, he called for "a sound climate of fiscal responsibility," urged the party to "unleash the creative forces," end "reckless deficits," exercise "compassion, leadership and restraint," to "build on the wisdom of our history," wage "the crusade against tyranny," to "revitalize," and "reconstitute," "reverse the accelerating drift" and "reclaim our legacy."

Bill will be more accessible, perhaps because he believes all the experts who stand around the lobbies saying that Bill is dead and the only thing left to do at this convention is to go to dinner.

In any case, Bill can usually be seen before cameras at the Hilton, saying that the platform is being "rigged," suggesting that Barry is dangerous and exuding optimism about his own

193

chances. Later General Eisenhower will come and smile on everyone, and Bill and Barry will congratulate each other as splendid fighters, and everyone will go to dinner and brag about the size of their checks.

As a convention, it may be short on drama, but isn't this a lovely city?

San Francisco-II

It is eerie here on the brink of the San Andreas Fault.

Resigned men in three-button suits wander through the fog predicting earthquake and looking for oriental strip-tease domes. At dawn on Nob Hill the Great Cowboy wakes from dreams of fiscal integrity and chats with Australia by short-wave radio.

Recently there was a great commotion about German journalism. Hundreds of people swarmed into small rooms to debate what the Great Cowboy had told Der Spiegel of wars past, present and future. The Cowboy told everybody to buy a copy of Der Spiegel and find out, but before anybody could find a Teutonic newsstand there was another literary sensation.

This occurred when the Tenderfoot from Back East sent the Great Cowboy a letter full of lively metaphor about plucked chickens and wrung necks. The corral set said their leader was so cross he forgot his call letters.

People who wear odd hats also became very cross with the dude and said that nobody could refer to them as plucked chickens. Finally the fellow from Back East said he had put his tenderfoot in his mouth, all right, but that he hadn't written the letter, and would have used a more delicate style if he had.

These literary squabbles possess the shabby men who crowd together in hotel lobbies and small rooms and scribble in notebooks. The shabby men are highly strung. They are fearful that the Great Cowboy will accuse them of being unfair. Sometimes one of them will approach another, take out his notebook, and ask, "Do you think you can be fair to the Great Cowboy?"

Sometimes the people who wear funny hats hoot at the shabby men and ask them why they do not scribble the truth about the Cowboy.

In the evenings thousands of people leave the city and reassemble in a large cattle shed in the suburbs, wearing their odd hats. There they are harangued about total victory and told that they can overthrow the Slick Rancher who occupies the Big Bunkhouse on the Potomac.

Afterward they wander about in the fog looking for Xanadus of strip-tease and tell each other, yes, the Slick Rancher can be overthrown, all right, if only they can stop thinking of each other as plucked chickens.

"We must bind up the wounds," they say, "and then everyone will see that the Slick Rancher's habit of turning out light bulbs is no substitute for total victory." At the cattle shed everyone is obsessed about light bulbs.

This is because they are drenched perpetually in blinding floods of light to illuminate the scene for cameras. These lights are like the lights used for the police third degree and no one can sit blinking into them for four hours without confessing to whatever the interrogators demand.

Afterward they go blinded into the fog truly believing that a man who can raise Australia by short wave radio can conquer a mere light-bulb squelcher.

Unfortunately, there are ghosts. Warren Harding's wanders the corridors of the Sheraton-Palace Hotel, murmuring that the state needs "equipoise" and "normalcy." Harding, the philosopher of the 1920's, died here. The defeated prince of petroleum from the East has the death suite, and Harding's shade feels put out.

You can feel it brush past in the lonelier corridors at cocktail time, headed doubtless for the local Xanadu, smiling its charming lady-killer smile. It does not commune about the Cowboy, or the Prince, or the Tenderfoot, or Der Spiegel, but it is very high on San Francisco.

If properly invoked while setting off in the fog to look for an oriental strip-tease dome, it will confide, "If ghosthood is your fate, San Francisco is the only town to meet it in."

Our failing scolds

This is the season of the angry-letter writers. Presidential campaigns bring them out in battalions. At this very moment, all over the country, thousands of them are slashing furiously at their stationery, drafting polemics, which they will send to editors for publication.

If read in large doses, these letters affect the spirits like a week of rain. It is not that the world they come from is such an alarming place, but that it is such a tired one. From year to year, from election to election, nothing ever seems to change in it, and the wonder is that the monotony never seems to overpower the angry-letter writer's high temper.

And yet it does not. The angry-letter writer is constantly "sick and tired" or "amazed and disgusted." One thing that sickens and tires him is "the tripe" that appears in the editor's newspaper.

It is an article of faith with him that "the tripe" emanates from "the sewer," or "the festering sewer," which is inhabited by the editor and his employes.

When not dismayed by tripe and sewers, the angry-letter writer spends his time fearing to think of our future. His world is always "beset," usually by twin sets of evils. "Anarchy and lawlessness," "chaos and confusion," "hatemongers and racists," and "cronies and cohorts" not only "beset" his world but also make him "dread to think of our future" and convince him that "our days of freedom are numbered unless."

It is the "unless" that makes his world tolerable, for it

196

embraces the possibility that the people will come to their senses and elect the right man, adopt the right policy on water fluoridation or remember what George Washington once said.

There are some good things in the angry-letter writer's world, but not many. One is "the two-party system." Others are "every thinking person" and "reasonable men." Every thinking person and reasonable men, along with the two-party system, are the last hope of "the republican form of government."

Every thinking person, naturally, knows that the Founders meant the United States to be a "republican form of government" and not "a democracy." Those who "through naiveté *or worse*" want to turn this country into a democracy are responsible for "the civil wrongs bill."

"Naiveté *or worse*" is one of the greatest menaces in the angry-letter writer's world. Other evils frequently invoked are "the wishy-washy attitude," "hysteria," "witch hunters," "king makers," "the red pestilence," "moguls and panjandrums" and "bureaucrats."

The places where all these evils reside are the dreaded "hotbeds"—"hotbeds of corruption," "hotbeds of conservatism," "hotbeds of red pestilence," etc.

Why is the country blinded to the perils of the hotbeds? Because of "distortion and innuendo." Why is Senator Goldwater or President Johnson, as the case may be, the man who does not make the angry-letter writer "sick and tired"? Because he has "intestinal fortitude."

The country deserves better from its angry-letter writers. The world they are describing is the same world their grandfathers wrote angry letters about forty years ago. They are letting the country down.

At a time when we need all the angry men we can lay hands on, they offer us the same old sick and tired, amazed and disgusted scolds of hotbeds, cronies and cohorts, king makers and naiveté *or worse* that have been berating us for generations.

They owe it to their country to face up to the 1960's and give us some real anger with a new slant. Reasonable men

197

will be amazed and disgusted at the wishy-washy attitude of today's angry-letter writers who, with their cronies and cohorts, out of naiveté *or worse,* lack the intestinal fortitude to lift the angry-letter readers out of the hotbeds of indifference.

The country is sick and tired of their failure. It will be long remembered. Our days of freedom are numbered unless something is done to restore the angry letter to the role that the Founders unarguably envisioned for it.

How the press was lost

Donald E. Lukens, the president of the National Federation of Young Republicans, must be a very young Republican indeed. Only the very young and very innocent could seriously propose, as Mr. Lukens has done, that the Young Republicans undertake a ten-year program to infiltrate the press and suffuse it with Republicanism.

Mr. Lukens is suggesting that up to one hundred young stalwarts should be slipped into what he considers enemy ranks. He seems to think that within ten years enough of these agents will become commentators, columnists and editorialists to make the news juicier reading for Republicans.

Mr. Lukens cannot possibly have thought this proposition all the way through. Let us take a hypothetical volunteer for the press infiltration corps. Call him Don. Don has just graduated from Yale and, through his fraternity connections, has lined up a good banking job in Wall Street.

By playing it safe, he may become a vice president in ten years, but being a dedicated Young Republican, he decides to chuck it all and join the press infiltration corps. With luck, he is offered a job at $75 a week to start and a guarantee of $150 after five years.

Does he start commentating, columning and editorializing immediately? He does not. He is ordered to go sit in police stations and leave the city editor alone unless he hears of a thug opening somebody's skull.

For a year or two Don sits around with the cops, learning poker and pool. On bad nights, he has to annoy dead children's parents for snapshots, get the Police Commissioner out of bed, and sit in accident wards listening to people die.

He begins to take on the coloration of his environment. His Yale suit needs pressing, and wherever he goes he gives off the sharp unmistakable smell of police stations.

He starts sitting in saloons listening to the tired confessions of striptease girls and sipping beer with bookmakers.

One day Don drops by the Yale Club and is barred at the door until his chief, Mr. Lukens, vouches for his character. There he sees his old classmates, who are discussing their trips to Europe and their adventures on the Big Board.

"That's old Don," they whisper to one another. "Smells like he's just got out of jail." "I hear he's been seen talking to floozies and drinking with bookmakers." "A pity." "Yes, and he was such a good Republican at Yale, too." Later, Don's fiancée will ask him to meet her someplace inconspicuous. She will tell him she can no longer wait and plans to marry his fraternity brother, Harry, who is doing so well at Chase Manhattan.

Finally, however, Don is promoted off the police beat to general assignments. He spends the next four years eating creamed chicken at banquets of washing-machine salesmen's conventions, and sitting under potted palms waiting for the after-dinner speakers to say something.

Night after night, week after week, year after year, they say the same thing: We live in perilous times. We must keep the faith in America and in the washing-machine industry.

One day Don is assigned to cover the wedding of an aging Young Republican classmate who is making a fortune in electronics. He is thrown out of the reception on orders from the bride's father, who has heard from Donald E. Lukens that all newspapermen are Democrats.

After six years inside enemy ranks, Don is at last told that he is ready for something big. "Washington?" he asks.

199

"Commentating? Columning? Editorializing?" "Nonsense," says the city editor. "You are our flood expert."

Covering his first flood, Don has his only suit ruined. To recover part of the loss, he bills his paper for a pair of hip boots, listing them as "essential to flood coverage." His auditor agrees to pay, but only if Don turns the hip boots in to the accountant's office.

After ten years inside enemy ranks, the big break finally comes. Don is sent to the Republican convention. He is manhandled by the police and jeered by the delegates. Donald E. Lukens, who has just been nominated for President, grants him an off-the-record interview to tell him how to report his acceptance speech.

Don punches Mr. Lukens in the nose.

It won't work, Mr. Lukens.

At grips with the issues

Senator Braithwaite, the outcumbent standard-bearer, challenged his incumbent opponent, President President, to tell the nation the truth.

When President retaliated by calling Braithwaite a "ranting, raving demagogue," Braithwaite backlashed by calling President a "liar," whereupon President President instructed the Ministry of Deterrence to hold a press showing of the ultra-secret S-2 Sky Poisoner.

Editor Omnibus thereupon chided both standard-bearers for immaterial conduct and cautioned them to stick to the issues. President President, obviously chastened, made headlines by walking fifteen times around the White House lawn, thus demonstrating with responsible restraint that the nation could count upon a firm gait to bear the finger to the trigger.

Alarmed by polls showing that sixty-one per cent thought

his trigger-finger too itchy, Braithwaite arranged for a televised appointment with the revered General Trelawney, and while the usual anesthetized millions watched at home, complained that President's well-poisoners were calling him a warmonger.

General Trelawney said it was "poppycock" to think that Harry Braithwaite would monger war, and Braithwaite said that, personally, he had always thought Trelawney had mongered the ideal foreign policy, even though he had once thoughtlessly taxed the old gentleman with running a "dime-store New Deal."

President President flew to the borders of Canada and Mexico to be photographed looking responsible, then flew to Texas to be photographed astride a responsible horse. Bishop Tallow of the historic Old Dean Rectory was photographed by Newsweek after urging his congregation to cast write-in ballots for President President's horse which, he sermonized, was the only sane and ethical creature he had seen photographed since the campaign's opening.

White House press secretary Jim Mimeo declined comment when asked whether the horse met constitutional qualifications for the Presidency. Cato Candy, leader of the ultra-humorless John Ultra Society, ordered his membership to deluge Editor Omnibus with poison-pen letters noting the conspiratorial role of the horse in the sellout of China.

Senator Braithwaite, meanwhile, took heart when "Pitchfork" Brimstone, the grand old angry man of the swamps, announced that he was switching his allegiance from the White Sheet Division of President President's party to support the Braithwaite campaign.

Editor Omnibus said this showed that whatever might be said against Brimstone, no one could charge him with lack of integrity. Senator Braithwaite ignored as beneath contempt allegations that Brimstone was the voice of the Ku Klux Klan. He contented himself with observing that Brimstone, who had run so well as the Okracrat candidate for President in 1948, would help immeasurably in precincts with a pressing alligator problem.

Fighting back, President President announced that, if re-elected, he would make it cheaper for women to buy jewelry, lipstick and handbags. Immediately, Maurice Henbane, Vice-Presidential candidate on the Braithwaite ticket, a man noted for his skill at making President President climb the wall, announced that nobody loved President President.

What's more, declared Henbane, President President had a house deed which forbade resale to Negroes, which showed that President was at heart just a Brimstone without integrity. Senator Braithwaite, meanwhile, had flown to Albany to be photographed with his arch enemy, Governor Blintz. Blintz declared Braithwaite's integrity impeccable and declined to re-open his former case against the condition of Braithwaite's trigger finger.

The polls indicated that most people would gladly vote at once if the campaign could be brought to a merciful close. Sensible people deplored the suggestion. To paraphrase James Thurber, democracy must be served—frequently stuffed.

The tiger who wouldn't roar

ABOARD GOLDWATER CAMPAIGN TRAIN, Sept. 30, 1964 —On the first day it was like this:

Town: Marietta, Ohio. Weather: gray and drizzling. The train had stopped beside the brown brick lump of a trackside hotel. ("A modern hotel. Rooms from $2. Since 1900.") Somebody with brass lungs stood on the back platform telling the crowd that Barry Goldwater "needs Randy Metcalf in Congress," and out on the fringes a gray-haired woman was chastising seven little girls who had brought placards advertising Lyndon Johnson.

"You just think about corruption in government," the woman was saying. "It's bad to have a corrupt man in government. Just think of that." Then, turning to another woman: "They might as well be for Al Capone." Harsh talk, but no harsher than many of the heckling signs which sprouted from the crowd as Senator Goldwater emerged from his private car.

"I'm too young to die," one read. And, "Goldwater for violence and poverty," "Barry loves bombs," "Help AUH₂O stamp out peace." Senator Goldwater was glad to be in Marietta, "the oldest city in the Northwest Territory," and after plugging the local candidates he declared himself for Social Security, denounced crime, promised the teen-agers that he would never let them be brought to war and ticked off President Johnson.

Every time Republicans raised a question, he said, Mr. Johnson went out to dedicate a dam. "But we have more questions than he has dams," he said. Part of the crowd laughed. The candidate introduced his wife and warned the crowd away from the tracks—"Voters are too hard to get to run over"—and the train creaked westward toward Athens.

At Athens the drizzle had stopped but the hecklers were thicker. "Even Johnson is better than Goldwater," one big placard read. Others linked his name to Hitler's and illustrated it with skull and crossbones.

Clearly annoyed by the hecklers' attempts to draw him as the war candidate, he tried to explain, "particularly for the teen-agers," that he advocated strength only to preserve the peace. He speaks in the calm, almost gentle cadences of the neighbor sipping a beer on the back porch, but the soothing effect is diluted by his penchant for powerful statements, and in the next breath he was telling the crowd it should be worrying about World War IV.

"We are at war today," he said, suggesting that World War III was already upon us in Vietnam. "If it weren't for you young people," he went on, "I would have quit politics long ago." "You should have!" shouted a heckler. The Senator introduced his wife and the train creaked westward—to Chillicothe.

At Chillicothe the crowd was big, sympathetic and ready

203

for rousing, but the Senator's genial backporch manner lacks the magic that turns crowds into roused rabble, and he gave them an eight-minute speech touching on ten major issues from war to welfare. These were his people, but he is more Scattergood Baines than the man on horseback, and he throttles their enthusiasm with gentle confusion.

He introduced his wife, and the train creaked westward to Blanchester, birthplace of Representative Clarence J. Brown, whose service in the House of Representatives dates from the pre-Cambrian age. Looking down on the station's red brick platform, the Ohio Lycurgus recalled when he had cleaned the bank cuspidors up the street sixty years ago and, blinking his eyes but finding not a sob in him, introduced Senator Goldwater to "the finest people on this old earth of ours."

Mr. Goldwater plugged "Ollie" and "Clarence," then produced a brown notebook and began reading quotations from the works of Hubert H. Humphrey. Senator Humphrey, he suggested in his gentle way, was an abysmal fellow who wanted Communist China in the United Nations and a socialist economy in the United States.

These were Clarence Brown's people, and the candidate explained that he was warning them against Hubert Humphrey because Mr. Brown had told him that that was what they wanted to be warned against. The problem, of course, was that in his gentle way Senator Goldwater really provoked no excess of passion against Humphrey. One suspected, in fact, that he might not be above a bout of gentle good fellowship with Humphrey back in the Senate Dining Room except for the exigencies of the campaign.

The Senator introduced his wife and said farewell to Blanchester and the train creaked toward safe Republican harbor in Cincinnati. It had not been a bad day, but it was scarcely a triumph.

It had also illuminated the Goldwater dilemma. His opponents have labeled him dangerous, but his gentleness reduces the roar of his ghost writers to a purr and stokes no fire in the glands of any but the most devout.

The rail campaign

ABOARD GOLDWATER CAMPAIGN TRAIN, Oct. 3, 1964—
This is the strangest way to make a President. What they
did, you see, was to put two hundred people on this peculiar
train and haul the thing over the Appalachians and then
drag it slowly through hundreds and hundreds of miles of
cornfields.

It must have been last Monday that it started. Or was it
the Monday before last? It is hard to be sure. Time gets away
from you in this compartment. Days seem like weeks. It may
be the creak of the wheels, or maybe the cigar smoke. The air
is very bad. It is hard to think clearly—.

Well, in any case, it is the strangest thing. The train rolls
through the cornfields while the politicians sit inside drinking
coffee and listening to "The Stars and Stripes Forever" on
squawk boxes. Every hour or so, the thing stops and all the
coffee-soaked politicians are put off and another shift is put
aboard.

Everybody else jumps off the train and runs to the rear.
The man who wants to be President comes out the back
door, and everybody shouts, "We want Barry, we want
Barry, we want Barry." "Well, you have him," says the
man who wants to be President, and the crowd laughs. There
is something very curious about this crowd. The faces never
change. The train rolls through a hundred miles of cornfields and there, lo and behold, is the same crowd that wanted
Barry at the last town. The woman carrying the sleeping
baby, the old fellow with leathery ears, the jeering adolescent
with L.B.J. placard. Always the same.

All day long this crowd keeps reappearing at the back of
the train and shouting "We want Barry" and laughing when
Barry says, "Well, you have him." Barry then warns about
the "curious crew."

The "curious crew" is not the train crew. It is a group of
people led by the other man who wants to be President.

205

Sometimes Barry calls them by funny nicknames—Yo-yo Mc-Namara, the Secretary of Defense, and Orville Wrong, the Secretary of Agriculture, for example. This really makes the crowd howl.

Afterwards, everybody runs back along the tracks and jumps aboard the train and drinks coffee while it runs through the cornfields playing "The Stars and Stripes Forever." It is a very long train—seventeen or eighteen cars—and people keep walking from one end to the other asking each other silly questions.

"How do you think he's doing?" is a very popular question. People who don't want Barry say he is doing badly, while people who do want him say the crowds have been great all day. It is impossible to ask Barry how he thinks he's doing, for he never appears outside the car with the coffee-drinking politicians and maintains only the most formal relations with the rest of the train.

The other day—was it in Indiana or Ohio?—he put on an engineer's hat and went forward to drive the train a while. He drives a train very smoothly. Should he fail to become President he would certainly make an adequate train driver.

It is odd. This sort of campaign gives a man an opportunity to demonstrate what kind of engineer he would be, but no chance to show how well he can run the country. As Barry might say, it is "curious."

Ah, the train is stopping again. This must be Mattoon, Ill., or perhaps Hammond, Ind. The last shift of local politicians is disembarking and the new one is getting on. Everyone is racing to the back. The crowd is at it again, shouting, "We want Barry." Barry is saying, "Well, you have him." The crowd is laughing. That eerie crowd. There is the woman carrying the sleeping baby. There is the old fellow with leathery ears. Could we be carrying this crowd in the baggage car?

Sometimes even Barry seems not quite real. In Indiana the other morning—or was it in Ohio last month?—he hailed the local Colgate toothpaste plant and declared that, if Government would stop harassing teen-agers and young married people, "there can be millions of these Colgates started

206

across the country." A man afterwards kept walking through the train asking where the country would get enough teeth to keep them all in business, but he was finally restrained and advised to go easy on the coffee.

It is curious here. Very curious. One has these fantasies, especially after nightfall. Perhaps it is the coffee and too much "Stars and Stripes Forever," but one has the gnawing suspicion that we are all doomed on this train.

Doomed to roll forever through the cornfields, listening to Barry say, "Well, you have him," seeing the old man with leathery ears day after day, week after week, year after year. And at night there are the dreams. Millions of toothpaste factories turning out billions of toothpaste tubes. It is a curious way to make a President.

The air campaign

ALBUQUERQUE, N. M. Oct. 28, 1964—It is hard to keep a clear head when you are caught inside a Presidential campaign.

From the outside, reading the headlines and watching television, it all seems so tidy. Barry says Lyndon believes in "daddyism." Lyndon says Barry is not fit to sit at the Washington end of the hot line. Neatly rounded-off crowds of thirty, fifty or a hundred thousand line routes, cheer, sulk, boo, clutch happily at candidatorial hands.

From a distance it looks crisp, exciting, cleanly dramatic. From inside it is something else. After twelve hours on the campaign plane, a simple recounting of what has happened sounds like a tale told by a madman. Well, to get to the point——

We left Washington at 3, were in Boston at 4 P.M. This, in itself, was ridiculous. It should take three hours at least to reach Boston and eight if you travel like a gentleman. This miracle of transportation is made possible by the jetliner, a

207

kerosene-powered restaurant which feeds and oils one hundred fifteen campaigners at altitudes above thirty thousand feet while annihilating time.

At Logan Airport in Boston in an apricot sunlight, politicians in black politicians' suits stroked cigars, shook hands and asked reporters to spell their names right while a band played "Mary Ann," a tune of the islands. The President's plane arrived. The President debarked to girlish squeals, was visible briefly in the bustle.

President, black-suited politicans and campaigners crushed into limousines and buses raced into Boston with brakes screeching, horns blowing, drivers cursing, and debouched among a herd of neighing police horses in Post Office Square. A crowd that may have been fifty thousand or three hundred fifty thousand as announced by the chief policeman murmured incoherently in the dark granite canyons.

The President began reading a prepared speech. The amplifiers failed, making it impossible to hear what he said. A woman screamed, fainted and had to be rescued by ambulance crews.

"You'd better get out of here before this crowd breaks through the police lines," advised a local policeman.

Everybody crushed into limousines and buses and raced to Logan Airport. The restaurant headed for Pittsburgh, food and oil flowing freely. Somewhere over Connecticut, or maybe New York, airborne policemen apprehended a man near the rear galley who announced that he was Chief Osceola of the Seminoles with a vital message for President Johnson.

Large crowds pressed to the rear galley to stare at the fellow. Stewardesses urged everyone to return to his seat to restore the restaurant's equilibrium. We all descended at Pittsburgh.

More politicians in black suits. More limousines and buses. More brake-screeching, horn-blowing, cursing. President lost to view. Crowds, if any, invisible in Pennsylvania night. Everybody filed into a huge dome where for one hour and four minutes the President spoke of absolutely everything while girls squealed and the mind reeled.

We all dashed back to our limousines and buses, raced to the airport. Brakes screeching, horns blowing, drivers cursing. The great restaurant soared through the vast moonless American night toward Evansville, Ind. Stewardesses of great loveliness served peanuts, olives and pickles. White House aides distributed mimeographed copies of speeches the President had made in Boston and Pittsburgh, speeches the President would make in Evansville, Albuquerque, Los Angeles.

The restaurant descended at Evansville in a shower of peanuts. The Evansville airport was dark and full of policemen looming out of the night with big gun holsters. Orion hung low on the horizon, snickering. From a great distance in a small harsh glare the President was visible. He said there were thirty thousand people listening to him out in that darkness.

The restaurant swished up over the Ohio River and high out across the plains and desert for Albuquerque. It was 1 o'clock in the morning when it took off and the stewardesses were serving steak.

In the twelve hours since leaving Washington the President had campaigned effectively across the length of the continent, someone said. Without newspapers or television it is hard to say here precisely what, if anything, happened.

Unseeing from coast to coast

WASHINGTON, Oct. 31, 1964—What a strange country this must seem to a Presidential candidate. He careens from one coast to the other but never walks on a beach, gazes at the sea or has time to study a wild flower.

He visits hundreds of towns and cities but his view is blocked by barriers of policemen and walls of cheering human flesh. He enters and leaves a hundred hotels seeing nothing but hands and smiles. He travels five thousand miles in a day, often seeing nothing but clouds, crowds and airport hangars.

To him, the sound of America is the wail of police sirens, the echo of his voice from bad amplifying systems, the roar of jet engines, the blare of high school bands and the hysteria of massed children celebrating a break in the school tedium.

In this strange America of the supercelebrity, there is no loneliness and no quiet. There are no still meadows for wool gathering, no empty city streets to walk at night, no deserts or prairies to make the mind wander, no dark country roads, no breathless mountain mornings.

In a single week President Johnson has made the equivalent of three transcontinental trips, traveling from Florida to Boston to Los Angeles to Philadelphia to Chicago to New York. In six days, his mileage has probably exceeded the lifetime travels of Lewis and Clark.

What did he see? What did he learn first hand about the country? That the foliage is still brilliant in New England and the Middle West, and that the Rockies are dusted with first snows of winter. This much was visible from his airplane window, but from the ground the view was much less conclusive.

In Boston he might have noted that the airport runway lights are red at night, that the police force favors horses for crowd control and that "Olga's House of Shame" ("36 Hours of Terror") was playing in a downtown movie house.

In Pittsburgh he saw skyscrapers shining in the night. If he glanced from his plane window before landing it might have occurred to him that while American cities are hideous by day, they are beautiful after sunset when only the lights are visible.

At Evansville, Ind., he could have noted only that the airport runway lights are blue, but at Albuquerque, N. M., he must have observed that the air is just as crisp at 9 A.M. as it is at 1:30 in the morning.

In Los Angeles he must have seen the smog, of course, and the superhighways which crisscross the town. If he happened to glance over the crowd once or twice, he might have noticed that Los Angeles is also the home of the Big Dough-Nut Drivein, the Oh-Boy Burger and the Merry-Go-Hound hotdog stand which is shaped like a carrousel.

San Diego was klieg lights in his eyes at the airport. Wichita was bright sunlight at the airport. The land is very flat at Wichita. Salt Lake City gave him a quiet look at the desert under his wings and, at breakfast time, a chance to test the famous acoustics of its tabernacle.

The Wasatch Range was lovely as he crossed it at five hundred miles an hour, but it is doubtful that he had time to ponder the hardship of the first Mormons who crossed it on foot pulling their homes over the ridges on two-wheel wagons.

Philadelphia at dusk smelled of chemicals and flaunted her policemen before him, but it is doubtful that he soaked up much of the local flavor. Anyone but a President could have strolled out of the hotel in midevening, asked the police for directions to a certain street, been told, "better hang on to your wallet," and felt suddenly that he had learned something worthwhile about Philadelphia.

Such advantages are denied to Presidential candidates. The irony of Presidential campaigning is that the candidates are condemned to travel the country incessantly but sealed off from every opportunity to discover it.

They find themselves exalted by a country which they may feel in their bones but they can never commune with it again until fame sets them free.

A glimpse of mercy

WASHINGTON, Nov. 7, 1964—At 10:45 on election night when it was apparent that the Great Society was upon us, the children were still too excited to sleep. "Tell us," they pleaded, "what it will be like in the Great Society."

For that fleeting instant, the vision was clear and the answer easy. "The Great Society, children, will begin in a burst of goodwill. Any minute now Senator Goldwater will come on television to congratulate President Johnson and he will smile gallantly and say, 'Even Strom Thurmond could have carried Alabama.'

"And then Walter Cronkite and Chet Huntley and three hundred political writers will all look at the Michigan returns and see that George Romney has been re-elected, and not one of them will say or write that George Romney has become an important contender for the Republican nomination in 1968."

"Why won't they say that, Daddy?"

"Because, son, in the Great Society we will no longer be subject to harsh and unjust punishment like a four-year sentence to Presidential politicking."

"What will Richard Nixon do in the Great Society?"

"Mr. Nixon will call a press conference, darling, and he will say that Governor Rockefeller is a great and good Republican. Governor Rockefeller will then reply that Mr. Nixon is a first-class fellow and will invite the Nixons to come by some evening for bridge."

"Will George Romney call a press conference, Dad?"

"Yes, George Romney will call a press conference, son, but no reporters will go. The reporters will call Mr. Romney and explain that in the Great Society the public needs time to think about football and housekeeping without political distractions."

"Will there be a place for Governor Scranton in the Great Society?" "Indeed there will, sweetheart. In the great day we're talking about, General Eisenhower will have his telephone disconnected and no Republican will be able to call him for one of those puzzling statements that we always argue about at dinner. And then he'll invite Mr. Romney and Mr. Nixon and Mr. Rockefeller down to the farm where nobody can reach them and where we won't have to think about them again for three years and six months. And he'll invite Governor Scranton too."

212

"Oh, Daddy, the Great Society is going to be wonderful. Tell us about Bobby."

"Well, son, when Bobby goes down to the Great Society Senate, he will put aside his speech writers and his campaign directors and he'll start way down there at the bottom working on the District of Columbia Committee and helping the Rules Committee improve the bean soup in the Senate dining room and, without ever telling anybody about it, he'll start working to elect Hubert Humphrey President of the United States in 1972."

"Gee, I'll bet Mr. Humphrey is really looking forward to the Great Society."

"He sure is, darling. And do you know why? Because in the Great Society President Johnson will never invite him down to the LBJ ranch and put him in funny clothes and make him get on a funny horse in front of a lot of photographers."

"Will everybody feel humble in the Great Society, Dad?" "They certainly will, but the best part is that nobody will ever come right out and tell you he feels humble. In the Great Society politicians will no longer be arrogant about their humility."

"It sure sounds great, Dad, but will the conservatives like it?"

"The conservatives will be realistic. They will say, 'In Senator Goldwater we had the most attractive candidate available. We conservatives must blame ourselves for not agreeing on what conservatism is'."

The children slept sweetly, but by 11 P.M. the election had become a nightmare. The conservatives blamed Goldwater. President Johnson was publicly humble. Humphrey was earmarked for horseback. Bobby was smiling oddly. Nixon, Rockefeller, Romney and Scranton were whetting knives. Cronkite was saying that Romney had become a contender for 1968.

And now the children are cynics. "Tell us about the Great Society," they say, and wink among themselves.

213